Whatever were you thinking of, Captain?

A Handbook for Airline Passengers

Captain John L. Morton

To 'the other two Johns'

Contents

Preface

There is no doubt that pilots are proud of what they do; after all, anyone would get a kick out of having a £100 million-pound toy to play with, let alone the responsibility for up to 500 lives, occasionally resting on a split-second decision. However, conceit rarely raises its ugly head because pilots are trained to be self-critical, and every Captain has next to him an astute First Officer waiting for a command vacancy! There are periods in a pilot's career when, for a brief moment he thinks he knows everything, for example, when he completes his first solo, when he achieves his first thousand hours' experience, and so on. He is usually rapidly reminded how wrong he is. I was still learning when I reached retirement age.

Young pilots tend to talk 'shop' rather too much, to the boredom of those around them. However, as they mature, they realise that other subjects do exist and, if asked what they do, may well answer 'I travel in aluminium tubing.' The conversation usually turns rapidly to something else.

I have dedicated this book to 'the other two Johns', Captain John Lester and Captain John Olive. The three of us joined British European Airways (later to become part of British Airways) in 1956, and we were posted to Renfrew Airport, Glasgow, as Second Officers, to fly de Havilland Herons, the first co-pilots to replace Radio Officers. We operated scheduled services around the Highlands and Islands, including beach landings at Barra. We also covered an average of one flight a day on the Scottish Air Ambulance Service. We have been firm friends ever since. Many years later, Captain Lester became my boss as Flight Manager TriStar, DC-10 and Concorde. He flew Her Majesty the Queen upon several occasions and retired in 1988.

I am indebted to my colleague *figment* (Captain John Reed) for his talented cartoons. The portrait on the back cover is reproduced from a chalk drawing by a Malaysian artist.

John L Morton

The publisher would like to express gratitude to Brian Bristow, David Doak, Douglas Nicolson and Chris Weir for their assistance.

Introduction

When Orville Wright made the first sustained and controlled flight in a powered aircraft at Kittyhawk, North Carolina, on 17 December 1903, he remained airborne for twelve seconds. His 12hp Flyer 1 flew at a height of between 8 and 12 feet at from 30 to 35 miles per hour. So he covered about two and a half times the length of a Boeing 747 at the height its passengers sit when the aircraft is parked. Today, with scheduled flights frequently exceeding twelve hours and covering over 6000 miles non-stop, carrying more than 400 passengers, we have come a long way!

When the company was operating at its peak, a British Airways aircraft took off or landed somewhere in the World every thirty seconds of every day. BA is only one of hundreds of airlines operating all over the globe. At London Heathrow, the busiest international airport in the World, there is a steady stream of landings at the rate of one every one and a half minutes (the time it takes for the preceding aircraft to clear the runway), and a similar number of take-offs on the parallel runway. Some 72 million passengers used the airport in 2000. Every day 100,000 people cross the Atlantic by air, and countless more make both shorter and longer trips. In the United States, 8.25 million aircraft take off every year. To accommodate all these travellers a huge construction programme was needed, and at one time Heathrow was claimed to be the only building site with its own airport! Many of these passengers may not have any interest in the operation of their flight, providing they arrive safely and on time. This book is for those who do.

One aim of a good airline pilot should be that, as far as possible, his passengers should hardly be aware of going up, down or round a corner. Perhaps the general public's idea of a member of the profession is of a tall, suave young man, wearing dark glasses and staring into the wide blue yonder. They could not be more wrong. The author certainly does not fit that description. The profession, like any other, has individuals of all shapes and sizes. It even has old women of both sexes! Having introduced 'women', I must acknowledge the growing number of highly competent lady pilots. Probably the main reason there are not more of them is the lack of opportunity and the prohibitive cost of obtaining the basic training, before gaining enough experience to be employed by an airline. Unless any young person is sufficiently talented to gain sponsorship, the road to a Commercial Pilot's Licence is a long and expensive one, requiring real determination and stamina. Throughout this book I hope I may be forgiven for referring to a pilot by the pronoun he. It is most certainly intended to encompass both male and female pilots and is only used to avoid clumsy sentences.

This book first explains the way crews go about their work and the background to airline operations, including some technical aspects couched in understandable terms. It then follows the logical sequence of a flight from the planning stage to 'after-landing' chores, commenting on what goes through the Captain's mind and the sort of decisions he has to make. Occasionally it has been necessary to digress in order to include some point of interest or anecdote.

1

The Airlines and their Crews

R unning an airline can be very profitable; a Boeing 747 can generate up to £50,000 revenue per flying hour. However, the difference between that and operating at a huge loss may only be a few percentage points in load factor. Offering the right number of seats at the right frequency and the right departure times is a matter for deep market research and skilled judgement. It may not be possible to optimise these factors because of overcrowded airports and airways, or as a result of government restrictions. Reciprocal agreements between airlines and between their respective governments can be a matter of protracted negotiation. The difference between scheduled and charter operations is that, in the first case, the airline puts a flight in its timetable and hopes enough people and freight come along to make it profitable; in the latter, the flight is sold to a charterer, who may already be guaranteed a full load, or is prepared to advertise it widely. On the basis of close to 100% load factor, a charterer can offer lower fares. The market is competitive and the airline may have to rely on in-flight sales to make a profit of any sort out of the operation. I spent nine years specialising in charter work and reckoned that I was in charge of the fastest off-licence in Europe!

Another factor in charter operations is that the airline cannot cancel a flight, whereas in the case of a scheduled operation, it can. It has to be admitted that it is not unknown for an airline to cancel a flight or amalgamate it with another one, if the payload is uncommercial. It may be dressed up under another excuse, but it happens, to the considerable inconvenience of passengers. If a charter airline cannot provide an aircraft or crew, it 'wet leases' (hires both) from another company. There is a telex network for such purposes and bids are invited from all over the region. Offers may be made by an airline that has to position an aircraft empty, say from Switzerland to the U.K., and the price they suggest has to include such extra costs. It may still be the best offer available at the time. Picking up other charter airlines' work in this way can be quite profitable, but the bidders should not overdo it, because they may be in the reverse situation the next week!

Responsibilities

From the moment a Captain enters an aircraft with the intention of flight, he is entirely responsible for the safety and well-being of his passengers and crew and the operation of his aircraft within the law. His First Officer, though possibly less experienced, is held equally responsible. After safety comes the pilot's duty to his company to ensure the efficient operation of his aircraft, which is an extremely expensive piece of equipment to buy and to run. The purchase price new of a large modern jet airliner can be around £100 million and its operating costs upwards of £10,000 per hour. It needs to be flown within its certified limitations at all times, yet its commercial potential must also be exploited to the full.

On the back of the Flight Deck door is a certificate of Third Party Liability insurance cover. This can be up to U.S. $1000 million for each aircraft. It provides an indication of the Captain's responsibility in purely financial terms, let alone in human lives.

The airlines have a slogan: 'Safety is no accident.' This is always taken seriously, but occasionally a sense of humour creeps in. Many years ago, a certain Flight Manager had a full-length mirror installed in the crew room, with the caption 'This man is responsible for your safety' written above it. It was not long before the mirror was adorned with a picture of Haile Selassie grasping the handles of a huge ship's wheel.

The Cabin Crew have an important role to play in the safe operation of their aircraft. British law requires there to be at least one cabin attendant per fifty passengers. They are highly trained for eventualities that are most unlikely to occur. Because they are rarely called upon to do more than provide passenger briefing on safety factors, they can be used to act as hosts on behalf of the company, serving food and drink, selling duty-free goods. It is a demanding job – just remember that they walk all the way there and all the way back!

In the 1970s, the supply of pilots from the Royal Air Force began to dwindle and

British Airways set up a training school for carefully selected and talented young men and women, based at Hamble, near Southampton. Those who completed the course and joined the airline were soon known as 'hamsters'. There was a slight over-production of trained young pilots and a fair number had to accept the frustrating situation of not being immediately needed as First Officers. The Company did not want to lose its investment, however, and these young people were temporarily redeployed as Cabin Crew. They were readily accepted as such, but quickly acquired from Stewards and Stewardesses the nickname 'Nigels'!

The manufacturer of any airliner is required to demonstrate that all passengers can be evacuated safely in 90 seconds while using only half the available exits. The provision of slides, which deploy and inflate automatically at each door, facilitates this. Compare this with loading passengers in an orderly fashion, which takes around five seconds per person, or more than half an hour!

As a passenger, you may very occasionally be seriously delayed because the crew are 'out of hours'. This is not a matter of being difficult but one of complying with the law on Flight Time Limitations, laid down for everyone's safety. The number of hours any crew member can work depends on the time of day he starts and the number of take-offs and landings he is to make. Generally speaking, a twelve-hour day is the normal maximum for a one or two-sector duty, reduced if it starts at hours described as unsociable. Three or more sectors in a duty day reduce the total number of hours that can be scheduled. In the event of a delay, the Captain may use his discretion to extend the duty by up to three hours, but he must consult every member of the crew, including the Cabin Attendants, before he does so. The problem is that they may have to decide not that they are too tired now, but that they will be in ten hours' time! These decisions are always made in a responsible fashion. Of course, if the crew can be replaced, the company will do this, but this may not be possible away from their base. Minimum rest between duties is twelve hours. This can be reduced on a 'split duty' basis, if the total time does not exceed fourteen hours and at least five hours' break with horizontal rest facilities is provided. This can be useful commercially to provide a late evening service to a fairly close destination, with an early morning return.

Now that we have aircraft capable of flying up to fifteen hours without refuelling, it is necessary on such flights to provide a 'heavy' crew – extra Flight Deck and Cabin Crew who can take over while the others make use of bunk facilities. The Captain who accepts the aircraft by signing the Ship's Papers (the Load and Balance Sheet, Technical Log, etc.) is designated the Commander, and he must be at the controls for both take-off and landing, though he may be relieved of his duties during the cruise.

Duty hours

In most airlines the crews have an agreement for service which allows peaks of duties that are compensated by lighter schedules on either side, for example a maximum fifty duty-hour week but an eighty duty-hour fortnight. This flexibility is essential for the company to be able to fulfil its program, but it must ensure that the crews are suitably rested and fit to operate at all times. The average duty hours over longer periods may well be lower than for other employees, but the job is extremely exacting and involves the ultimate in working unsocial hours – very early or very late starts, swapping from night to day duties and accepting the effects of multiple time-zone changes. Though the aircraft is pressurised, crews are effectively working on top of a 6,000-foot mountain, affected by a slight amount of oxygen deprivation (see **Medical Factors** in Chapter 2). All crews are monitored for radio-activity doses, especially those on Concorde who fly at altitudes of around 60,000 feet, above the atmosphere's protective layers. It has been suggested that male crew members should wear lead-lined athletic supports.

Licensing and Training

There are quite rightly extensive laws governing aviation under the Air Navigation Act and Air Navigation Regulations. Naturally all pilots would wish to operate within the law. Rumour has it that in Jersey the law requiring all powered vehicles to be preceded by a man carrying a red flag has never been repealed. In the event of an industrial dispute and a work-to-rule, the pilots might find this useful.

There are three levels of licence which allow a pilot to fly for hire and reward. The Commercial Pilot's Licence permits the holder to fly as a Captain of small aircraft or as a second pilot of anything. A Senior Commercial Pilot's Licence increases the weight of the aircraft that may be flown in command, and an Airline Transport Pilot's Licence (ATPL) is without restriction. However, each licence has to be endorsed with the type of aircraft to be flown and qualification for this is by a written technical examination plus a flight test on each type. All of these are subject to validation by a medical examination, at least annually, and every six months for older pilots. A test is required for the issue of a Flight Radio-Telephony Operator's Licence, which is an essential adjunct. The basic licences are issued when the applicant has passed an examination and achieved the laid down level of flying experience. The ATPL examination requires a high standard of achievement in Aviation Law, Flight Instruments, Flight Planning, Meteorology and Climatology, Navigation, and the use of Radio Aids. Though administered by individual governments, the standards are internationally agreed. These are currently being harmonised under the Joint Aviation Authority (JAA).

An ATPL is not valid without an Instrument Rating (IR). Initially this involves a flight test on a multi-engined aircraft with one engine failed, conducted entirely on instruments. The exercises are quite difficult and entail precision flying to a high standard. The IR must be renewed annually. Also, every six months, each pilot is required to undertake a competency check, which is usually carried out on a flight simulator. These normally take two two-hour sessions and the syllabus, laid down by the company's Flight Training Manager with the approval of government authorities, varies each time, to incorporate all sorts of emergency procedures, sometimes using difficult situations actually experienced by the pilot's own airline or by others around the World. There is widespread international co-operation between the airlines on safety matters. Instrument Rating renewals, if required, are built into these checks.

Simulators are sophisticated computers consisting basically of a totally realistic flight deck on hydraulic rams, which give a fairly true feeling of motion in three dimensions. A complete range of exercises can be carried out, including, if necessary, a take-off, climb to cruise, descent and landing, but generally to save time are concentrated upon a particular phase or procedure. All of this can be completed entirely on instruments, but a visual facility in the form of a variable scene at night defined by individual lights is also provided, so that approaches to difficult airports can be demonstrated. Turbulence and wind changes can also be simulated, as can approaches with a low cloud base and/or poor visibility, so that the transition from instruments to visual flying can be practised.

Aer Lingus named some of their aircraft after saints. Their simulator was known as St. Thetic. One European airline commemorated famous explorers. The pilots christened the simulator Baron von Münchhausen, who, you may recall, was a gentleman who told very tall travellers' tales without actually ever going anywhere. Incidentally, it was rumoured that Swissair had considered the idea of naming their aircraft after famous Swiss heroes. On reflection, they thought it might be a bit confusing to have seventy-five aircraft all named 'William Tell'.

The cost of running simulators is a fraction of that of flying the aircraft themselves. For a pilot to convert from one aircraft type to another, he will typically spend some 40 hours in the simulator, before covering a few vital exercises on the aircraft itself. By this time he will be entirely familiar with the flight deck layout and routine procedures. Prior to this he will have spent some weeks in ground school learning how the aircraft systems work and their limitations. This will include a study of the engines and fuel management, electrics, pressurisation and air conditioning, hydraulics, and de-icing.

When he has completed this phase of his training, he will spend two to three weeks on the line under the supervision of Route Training Captain. He will run through a syllabus of exercises and be able to familiarise himself with the route pattern of his new aircraft, before being assessed as competent to operate as a normal crew member.

Once a year, each pilot is required to complete a Route Check. This is a routine line operation by a crew, with a Route Check Captain sitting in an extra seat in the Flight Deck but not taking any part in the conduct of the flight. He will debrief the crew afterwards, with comments intended to help and improve their performance and also to standardise the operation, so that any pilot can fly with any other knowing what to expect. Though it would be impractical on grounds of cost, I think that such a system extended to car drivers would greatly enhance road safety, preventing bad habits from developing.

One other annual training event, attended by pilots and Cabin Crew alike, is a refresher on the safety equipment carried on the aircraft – fire extinguishers, First Aid kits, lifejackets and dinghies, loudhailers, oxygen masks, etc.

Route experience

Before operating in command on any route, a Captain must comply with the route experience requirements for both his destination and alternates. The vast majority of airports (Category A) are straightforward and the Captain is permitted to brief himself, using the various charts available and notes provided by his company. The most difficult part of this is finding the toilets in the terminal building, as they are not shown on the aerodrome diagrams.

Category B airfields are slightly trickier and require the Captain to be briefed by another who is familiar with them and who has visited them recently. In some companies self-briefing is acceptable, using written notes including the aerodrome charts and approach diagrams. Category C fields, such as Gibraltar and the old Hong Kong Kai Tak, require a visit in a subordinate capacity. Destinations in the United States fall into Category C, by reason of certain operational factors and the language problem for English speakers! However, a visit to one qualifies the Captain for all of them.

Some time after I had left charter operations at Gatwick for scheduled work at Heathrow, I was offered a month's flying, helping with the summer peak on holiday charters again. One day, I was rostered to operate to Palma, an airfield placed in Category B because of the mountainous terrain to the north. I found that my recency had expired and I needed to be briefed by another Captain. Everybody fell about laughing, because I had been there 178 times.

Rostering

Flight Crew are usually rostered together for one duty cycle. This may be a single day's work on short-haul routes or two weeks or more on long-haul, where an integration may be quite complicated. This results in pilots having many acquaintances and very few friends in the profession, but it does lead to a wide experience of personalities. Flight Deck procedures are so standardised that there is no problem with strangers flying together, and, in the unlikely event of there being any friction between pilots, it does not have time to develop. With perhaps 300 pilots on the same aircraft type, it may be months before the same two fly together again. Cabin Crew are often on separate integrations, so may only fly under the same Captain for one duty period at a time, or may be with him for several consecutive ones. With a dozen or more of them on each aircraft, they probably work together even less often.

Short-haul crews may operate four or more sectors in a working day, for example to Paris and back twice. Although the total duty time may be under nine hours, it can be a very tiring day because of the intensity of the work. The actual flying time from London to Paris is 32 minutes, but packed into those is as much work as in perhaps a four-hour sector. There are one or two extraordinary operations, such as those island-hopping in the Orkney and Shetland islands. The sector from Westray to Papa Westray is scheduled to take two minutes. It is quite practicable for a crew to fly an out-and-back service from London to, say, Vienna, then take a flight out to Milan, nightstop there and return next day, popping over to Amsterdam and back for good value! This sort of intense operation may be repeated, then followed by two or three days off. Standby duties at the airport, to cover disrupted services or crews failing to report for duty without notice for whatever reason, can be very tedious, as all pilots would prefer their armchair to be airborne.

Many years ago crews had an agreement for service which allowed the company to insist on their flying outside the normal rostering rules (not the legal limitations), in extreme circumstances beyond the company's control. The company were required to issue a 'pink chit' (if you collected six, you qualified for a free tea set!), and the reasons for doing so were subsequently discussed at Head Office meetings with the union. One such chit was issued because of disruption caused by the

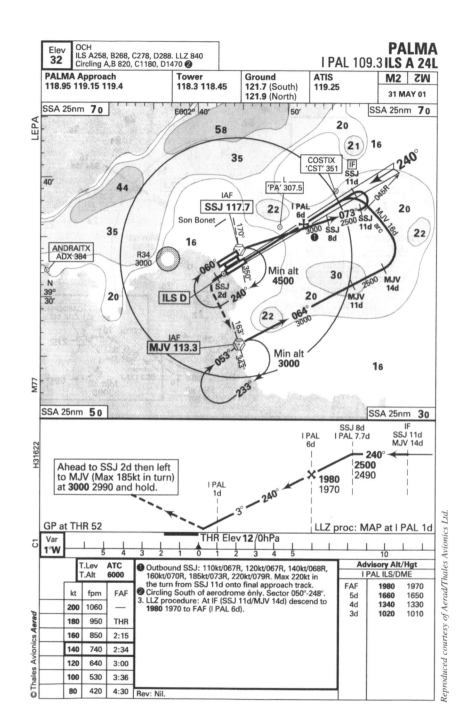

PALMA

I PAL 109.3 ILS A 24L

Elev 32	OCH ILS A258, B268, C278, D288. LLZ 840 Circling A,B 820, C1180, D1470 ❷				M2	ZW
PALMA Approach 118.95 119.15 119.4		**Tower** 118.3 118.45	**Ground** 121.7 (South) 121.9 (North)	**ATIS** 119.25	31 MAY 01	

Ahead to SSJ 2d then left to MJV (Max 185kt in turn) at **3000** 2990 and hold.

GP at THR 52

LLZ proc: MAP at I PAL 1d

THR Elev **12** /0hPa

Var **1°W**																	

	T.Lev **ATC** T.Alt **6000**	❶ Outbound SSJ: 110kt/067R, 120kt/067R, 140kt/068R, 160kt/070R, 185kt/073R, 220kt/079R. Max 220kt in the turn from SSJ 11d onto final approach track. ❷ Circling South of aerodrome only. Sector 050°-248°. 3. LLZ procedure: At IF (SSJ 11d/MJV 14d) descend to **1980** 1970 to FAF (I PAL 6d).	**Advisory Alt/Hgt** I PAL ILS/DME	
kt	fpm FAF		FAF	**1980** 1970
200	1060 —		5d	**1660** 1650
180	950 THR		4d	**1340** 1330
160	850 2:15		3d	**1020** 1010
140	740 2:34			
120	640 3:00			
100	530 3:36			
80	420 4:30	Rev: Nil.		

18

closure of Tel Aviv Airport for Yom Kippur. The union representatives felt this was not acceptable, because the Day of Atonement had been around for some 4000 years and the Company should have anticipated it!

Technical matters

The Technical Log provides the Captain with a history of the aircraft's engineering status. It also shows the fuel remaining from the previous flight, the amount loaded and the contents of the tanks ready for the next departure. It is an important legal document and therefore is to be taken seriously. However, from time to time, humour creeps in and some entries have achieved fame within the profession. The Vanguard aircraft was fitted with its own airstairs for passenger access. A Captain had entered in the Technical Log 'Front airstair creaking as if haunted'. The engineer's clearance stated 'Front airstair lubricated and exorcised'. Other classic entries included 'Left inside main tyre almost needs replacement' – 'Left inside main tyre almost replaced'; 'Something loose in the cockpit' – 'Something tightened in the cockpit'; 'Dead bugs on windshield' – 'Live bugs – nil spares available'; Number 3 engine missing' – 'Number 3 engine found on starboard wing after brief search', and many others.

There is so much redundancy built into modern aircraft that it is often possible to dispatch the flight with known technical deficiencies. The story goes that, when the TriStar was being built at Lockheed's factory in Burbank, the executive washroom had two toilet rolls in each cubicle, one marked MAIN and the other STANDBY; such was the thinking regarding built-in safety factors. The Captain has absolute discretion over taking so-called 'allowable deficiencies', though he has a book to guide him in his decisions. It may be that he is at an outstation and the only spares available are back at base. It would not be practicable to carry a large stock of spare parts at every station. However, there is a degree of co-operation between airlines, who borrow from each other's stores. The sort of deficiency a Captain might accept could be an engine-driven electric generator. There would be one on each engine and one on the auxiliary power unit, which is usable at low altitude, each capable of providing a substantial output. If the flight were to be a short one in daylight with good weather en route and at destination and alternate, there would probably be no reason to delay or cancel the flight.

The reliability of modern jet engines is such that there could be no justification in keeping spares all round the World, except perhaps at a few strategic places. Unplanned shutdowns (a euphemism for engine failures!) can occur as often as once every 600,000 flight hours, or, for an average use of an aircraft, about every forty years. Engines cost upwards of £6 million pounds each, which is a lot of money to have doing nothing. Spare engines can, if necessary, be ferried externally as an extra under-wing pod, from an engineering base to an outstation. An engine change need only take about four hours. Incidentally the engines are only held on to the wing by quite small-diameter bolts. This is in fact a built-in safety factor, because, should a failed bearing or lost fan blade cause severe vibration, the engine will drop away, rather than shake the wing off. It would admittedly be pretty unfortunate for people or property on the ground, but since 70% of the World's surface is ocean and huge areas of the land are uninhabited, the actual risk is very low indeed.

It is many years since electric adjustment to pilots' seat positions was introduced. Soon after it was, the advice opposite was published:

Some aircraft statistics
The Boeing 747-400 is the latest development of the first 747 rolled out on September 30, 1968. Since then over 1200 747s have been made in six different versions. The Flight Deck was placed high above the nose to allow for the possibility of access for freight via large doors in the front of the fuselage. There was a tongue-in-cheek suggestion that the Flight Deck would be better mounted in the tail, in the same way as the bridge is placed near the stern of some large ships, so that the pilots could see the whole aircraft in front of them and be able to place the wheels on the ground for landing, instead of having to feel their way down! This would not have done a lot for the streamlining of the aircraft!

The width of the fuselage was dictated by the requirement, in an all-freight version, to load two standard pallets side by side. The under-floor holds offer 1200 cubic metres of space, allowing for ten to twelve tonnes of cargo and/or 500 pieces

INTERNATIONAL AIRLINES
Installation of Flight Deck Electric Seat Adjustment

General:
When working in the Flight Deck, Powerseat circuit breakers on Panel S must be tripped, to prevent powering the seats accidentally. The motors on Powerseats operate at a high rate and may catch you in an awkward position.

Inadvertent Operation in Flight:
Determine which seat is running away. In flight it is possible to mistake which seat is at fault. If the Captain's seat is out of control forward, it will appear to the Captain that the First Officer's is running backwards. This is a common form of spacial disorientation and will only last until the Captain is emasculated on the control column. DO NOT disengage the autopilot at this time, as a violent pitch down will result. In order to determine which seat is the runaway, suggested procedure is to awaken the Flight Engineer for troubleshooting.

In cases of runaway seats, crew members have described noises of a low, rumbling nature, followed by the words 'My seat is – running - awaaay' and a piercing scream of increasing intensity and pitch, especially in forward runaways. As in all emergencies and in order to comply with Company Standard Procedures, the First Officer will silence the aural warning by clamping a hand over the Captain's mouth and advising 'Captain's mouth – Shut.' Subsequently refer to the checklist located on the underside of the Captain's seat cushion.

Should the seat run away in the forward mode, the ball-bearings will interlock and jam the seat when it is four inches from the instrument panel. The seat will then be stuck in the forward position, but begin travelling up in the vertical mode. The Captain will advise the crew 'I have jammed ballbearings.' The Flight Engineer will immediately refer to the CAPTAIN JAMMED BALLBEARINGS drill, located on the aft face of the rear freight hold bulkhead. It is imperative that the crew check for control column damage at this time. If the control column is broken, the Flight Engineer will inform Company Technical that the Captain has a fractured joystick and jammed ballbearings.

He should trip the port Powerseat circuit breaker on Panel S, to prevent the seat running up further in the vertical mode, which could cause the bearings to overheat. (The Captain's position will prevent him from monitoring this action). If this drill is delayed, a fire may start under the Captain, resulting in a CAPTAIN'S LOWER AFT BODY OVERHEAT. The Flight Engineer will advise the Captain of the fire and he will acknowledge this with 'Fire – my backside.'

Should the seat continue to run away in the vertical mode, the First Officer will advise the Captain 'Seat up, up, up.' The Captain will reply 'molejty vtds ftrkl.' It is suggested procedure to place a pillow at the Captain's head and land at the nearest available airport.

of baggage. The maximum weight of a 747–400 is just under 397 tonnes, of which the paint weighs half a tonne, equivalent to more than 500 family cars - supported on eighteen wheels. Normal seat configuration is for 420 passengers, for whose comfort there are nine galleys and fifteen toilets. A high-density layout for holiday charters can provide for 568. In total contravention of the law but during an emergency evacuation from their war-torn country, 1087 Ethiopian refugees were once uplifted in a 747 by El Al. The aircraft arrived with more passengers than it left, three babies having been born en route.

The 747 could be described as six million components flying in close formation. Its construction involves more than 1100 companies. It can carry around 47,718 imperial gallons of fuel, which will keep it airborne for more than fourteen hours, cruising at 575 miles per hour.

The next move up would seem to be the recently announced Airbus A380, designed to carry 555 passengers on two decks running the full length of the aircraft. There should be no technical reason why this should not be realistic, but there may be a few headaches on the ground, when it comes to providing boarding lounges and other facilities. Loading and unloading times could be excessive, though several doors will no doubt be used simultaneously. It will surely be necessary to have Disneyland-type queue control to have any chance of success.

Of course, for shorter routes on which more frequent services carrying fewer passengers are required, smaller aircraft are better suited and more economical. A reliable workhorse is the Boeing 737 (nicknamed the FLUF(f) – Funny Little Ugly Fella), which carries up to 126 passengers for 1,280 miles at 506 mph (Mach 0·74). The Airbus A320 can move a few more people a little faster for up to 2,000 miles. The Boeing 757 (called the Stick-insect, because it looks like one, when its undercarriage is down) takes up to 195 fare-payers some 2,300 miles, while in the charter world this can be increased to 235 passengers in the 'knees-under-your-chin and elbows-tucked-in' configuration. Its brother, the 767, which looks externally very similar, carries more farther. A very economical aircraft for long-haul routes is the Boeing 777, which can take 383 people 7,257 miles on only two engines. Concorde (the Bionic Pencil) is a very special case. It can carry only 100 passengers but cover 4,000 miles in three hours (Mach 2·0).

2

Background Matters

Air Traffic Control

Every country provides an Air Traffic Control (ATC) service, for which it makes a charge to airlines using it. Its job is to provide safe separation between aircraft and to pass relevant information to the pilots. Some less developed countries do not have radar coverage for all the airways and have to fall back on procedural separation between aircraft, which means that a greater distance (usually ten minutes' flying time) has to be allowed between consecutive flights at the same level, and climb or descent through opposing traffic can be subject to significant delays, awaiting the certainty that the aircraft have passed each other. Sometimes one-way airways are set up to avoid this problem. Flights are coordinated from and to neighbouring centres, usually by direct telephone line. The safety of his aircraft remains the responsibility of the Captain and he is not obliged to comply with Air Traffic Control directions. However, he would obviously have to have very good reason not to do so, because he might not have the whole picture of what is going on and they almost certainly would. Instead of the correct callsign 'London Tower', one American pilot amused us by addressing them as 'Tower of London'.

In the line of aircraft on the approach to an airport, it is necessary to ensure that there is a larger gap than normal behind a heavier one, because of the wake turbulence it generates. To assist ATC in this, bigger aircraft use the suffix 'heavy' after their radio call sign.

One notorious anecdote refers to a sizeable aircraft which had made its approach at rather too high a speed and used all of the runway for its roll-out. The Control Tower is reputed to have broadcast 'Clipper 104 Heavy, clear the runway via the last high-speed turn-off. If unable, take the Guadeloupe exit off Highway 103, hang a right at the lights and return to the airport.' Another classic, after an aircraft had become airborne a couple of times after the first touchdown, was 'Continue bouncing to the end, clear right and contact Ground Control on 121·9.' A nice one on take-off followed a report by the preceding aircraft that there was a dead animal on the runway. When asked by Control if they had copied the report, the reply from the next to take-off was 'Roger – we have already advised our caterers.'

Many years ago, the holding pattern for aircraft approaching London Heathrow was based on a radio facility at Watford, Hertfordshire. One day, the Chief Steward had just reported to the Captain that a passenger was locked in the toilet and was therefore not strapped in for landing. The Captain asked London Airways if he might delay his approach because he had an old lady locked in the lavatory. Without batting an eyelid, the controller replied, 'Roger; hold at Watford till Saturday.'

Because of the geographic spread of the language during and after the Second World War, all Air Traffic Control is conducted in English, except for the concession that domestic flights may use their own language. This is discouraged wherever possible, so that all pilots listening out can understand the traffic pattern. British pilots are, of course, lucky, in that we don't have to reach a level of fluency in another tongue. The standard has to be high, even though most messages are routine, and it must be quite difficult for, say, a Greek pilot to converse with Spanish ATC in English. On one occasion, when I was flying over northern Portugal, some confusion did occur, but fortunately it was of little consequence. We were approaching a line of thunderstorms and requested from ATC a clearance to go to port to avoid them. Some minutes later Lisbon Control, monitoring us on radar, asked us what we were doing going left, when Porto was to our right! It was our fault for expecting a foreigner to pick up a fairly obscure technical term in English.

Whenever contacting Air Traffic Control, the station being called is given first, followed by the aircraft's call sign (often the airline's prefix and the flight number). It is a nice courtesy to pass the time of day in the controller's own language, though the rest of the transmission would be in English. A standard position report consists of the aircraft callsign, the place just passed and the time over it (Greenwich Mean Time), the aircraft's flight level, and the estimated time for the next reporting point. For example: 'Athenai, kalispera, Speedbird 155, Thessaloniki at 1716, Flight Level three-three-zero, estimate Skopelos at 28.'

OK POLLY... TELL IBERIA 154
TO CLIMB TO FL 140····

An English phonetic alphabet was used for radio communication during World War II (Able, Baker, Charlie, Dog, etc.), but around 1955 it was realised that this was totally unsuitable for the rapidly-growing international civil aviation industry. A new alphabet was cleverly devised using English words which were often widely understood throughout the World and which could not be confused with others in the list, for example Mike and November. They also had to be words that were not obscene or otherwise unacceptable in other languages. It is therefore not surprising that a number of them have been adopted by motor-car manufacturers (Alpha, Bravo, Delta, Golf, Sierra). See **Appendix 2** for full details. Some of the more amorous younger pilots were known as Hotel Romeos!

Some difficulty may occur on airways, if a faster aircraft is catching up a slower one at the same Flight Level and no other levels are available. At altitude the density of the air is much lower than on the ground, and even though the true speed is quite high, the amount of air passing over the wings (as shown by the Indicated Airspeed) will not be enough to keep the aircraft from stalling, if it is slowed significantly. There is therefore only a small range of speed available. To turn a complete circle in order to lose time can take up to eight minutes at cruising level, because the bank angle has to be restricted to about 22° or the passengers will be subjected to unacceptable g forces. This is usually far too much time to lose, so the only alternative is to fly a dog-leg – turning off at an angle and returning to the airway centreline. Airways are normally only ten miles wide and it would only take a couple of minutes to reach the edge. The pilot has to consider whether he might

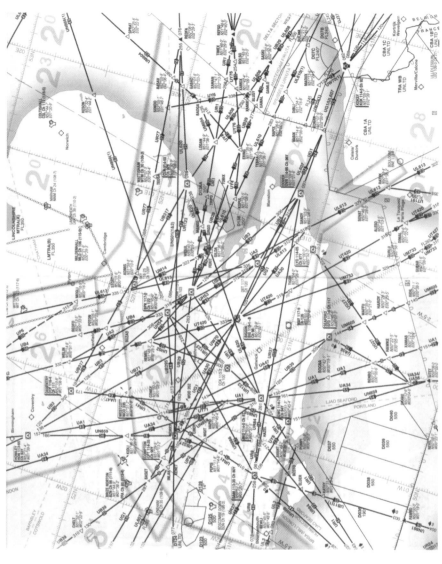

Air routes over the south-east of England.

Extracted from an En Route High Altitude map of the UK and Baltic Sea and reproduced courtesy of Aerad/Thales Avionics Ltd.

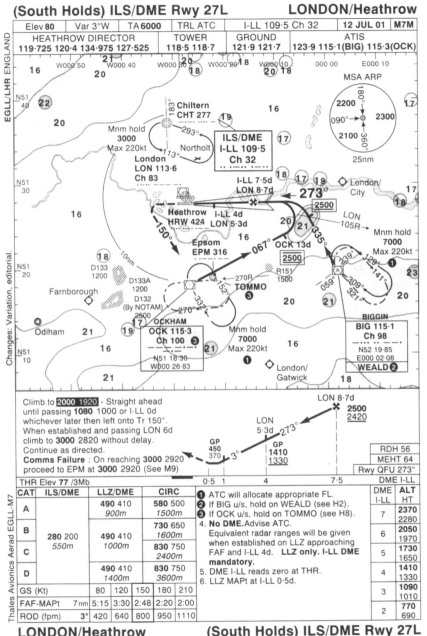

| Elev 80 | Var 3°W | TA 6000 | TRL ATC | I-LL 109·5 Ch 32 | 12 JUL 01 | M7M |

| HEATHROW DIRECTOR 119·725 120·4 134·975 127·525 | TOWER 118·5 118·7 | GROUND 121·9 121·7 | ATIS 123·9 115·1(BIG) 115·3(OCK) |

EGLL/LHR ENGLAND

W000 50   W000 40   W000 30   W000 20   W000 10   000 00   E000 10
16   20   (18)   8   (20) 18

MSA ARP

N51 40 (22)
20

183° Chiltern
CHT 277 (19)   16
Mnm hold 3000 293°
Max 220kt 113°
Northolt
London LON 113·6 Ch 83

ILS/DME (17)
I-LL 109·5
Ch 32

2200
090° → ⊙ ← 2300
2100 360°
25nm

N51 30
16
I-LL 7·5d (18) (17) (19)
LON 8·7d   273° ✶ 2500
London/City
17
(18)

Heathrow I-LL 4d
HRW 424 LON 5·3d
20 (21) 335°

Epsom EPM 316 067°
16 OCK 13d
2500
LON 105R →
Mnm hold 7000
Max 220kt

N51 20
(18) 10nm
D133 1200
D133A 1200
D132 (By NOTAM) 2500
Farnborough

270R
152° TOMMO (3)
R151 1500
299° 129° 141°
059° 309° 321°
(A) 23
20
(21)

OCKHAM
OCK 115·3
Ch 100 (3)
N51 18·30 W000 26·83

Mnm hold 7000
Max 220kt (21)
(1)
London/Gatwick

BIGGIN
BIG 115·1
Ch 98
N52 19·85
E000 02·08
WEALD (2)

Odiham 21 (19)
N51 10
16
21
16
18

Climb to **2000 1920** - Straight ahead until passing **1080** 1000 or I-LL 0d whichever later then left onto Tr 150°. When established and passing LON 6d climb to **3000** 2820 without delay. Continue as directed.
Comms Failure : On reaching **3000** 2920 proceed to EPM at **3000** 2920 (See M9)

LON 8·7d
✶ 2500
2420
LON 5·3d 273°
GP 450 370 3° GP 1410 1330

RDH 56
MEHT 64
Rwy QFU 273°

THR Elev 77 /3Mb					DME I-LL

CAT	ILS/DME	LLZ/DME	CIRC		DME	ALT
A		490 410 900m	580 500 1500m	① ATC will allocate appropriate FL.	I-LL	HT
B	280 200 550m	490 410 1000m	730 650 1600m	② If BIG u/s, hold on WEALD (see H2). ③ If OCK u/s, hold on TOMMO (see H8). 4. **No DME.** Advise ATC. Equivalent radar ranges will be given when established on LLZ approaching FAF and I-LL 4d. **LLZ only. I-LL DME mandatory.** 5. DME I-LL reads zero at THR. 6. LLZ MAPt at I-LL 0·5d.	7	2370 2280
C			830 750 2400m		6	2050 1970
D		490 410 1400m	830 750 3600m		5	1730 1650
					4	1410 1330
GS (Kt)	80	120	150	180	210		3	1090 1010
FAF-MAPt	7 nm	5:15	3:30	2:48	2:20	2:00		2	770 690
ROD (fpm)	3°	420	640	800	950	1110			

0·5 1 4 7·5

27

be straying into a military Danger Area or invading a hostile country's airspace, causing a diplomatic problem. This is where radar-controlled airways can come into their own – one aircraft can be cleared along a track on one side of the airway but still within it; the faster aircraft can be monitored as it maintains, say, five miles lateral separation along the other side.

Aircraft Registrations

Immediately after World War I it became clear that civil aircraft would need to be registered. In the United Kingdom a series began, using the numbers K-1, K-2, K-3, etc. It did not take long before it was obvious that the system would rapidly become unwieldy and a new scheme using letters was initiated in 1923. The letters G–E indicated an aircraft registered in Great Britain and were followed by three more letters. Registrations proceeded from G-EAAA to G–EBZZ, at which stage the whole thing started over again with G–AAAA, AAB, AAC, etc., and continued that way up to the present. We are well into the G–Cs. There were very few special out-of-sequence numbers until recent years, once of the first of these, G–BOAC, being allocated to an early Concorde. Now, as with private cars in the U.K., cherished registration numbers are allowed. Nearly every other country signed a convention to use a similar system of five-letter combinations, the one or two letters before the dash indicating the aircraft's nationality. France and Germany used F– and D– respectively, but many others do not seem to have a logical origin - OY– for Denmark, TF– for Iceland, VH– for Australia, etc. There are a few notable

exceptions - countries that did not sign the convention. The most prominent of these is the United States, which uses the letter N followed by digits and letters, the last of which sometimes indicate the operating airline. The USSR used CCCP followed by digits, but since the break-up of the Union most of the newly emerging countries in the Federation are using conventional five-letter combinations. Mainland China and Taiwan use B with a number of digits. See **Appendix 1** for full details.

For their own convenience, airlines refer to the aircraft in their fleets by the last two letters of their registration (Bravo X-ray, for example). These letters are usually painted on the nosewheel doors. The full registration appears on the rear fuselage.

Airports

For luggage labels, airports have three-letter codes. The derivation of most of these is obvious, but one in particular, that for Malaga, is interesting. In order to avoid confusion with Milan Malpensa and Malta the letters AGP were chosen. Why? Because in ancient Roman times there was a town there called Agrippina, the name of the mother of Nero. Some crew members tie labels for Singapore (SIN) on their briefcases, on the basis that it pays to advertise.

It may also be of interest that the name Gatwick derives from a goat dairy farm once sited close to the middle of today's runway, 'gat' being an old English word for 'goat'.

When I was a First Officer, I was walking through Milan Airport concourse with a quick-witted Captain, when we were approached by an Englishman, who had obviously spent a fortnight speaking demonstrative English to Italians. He pointed to himself, then to some cases, then to a corner of the concourse, saying 'Can - I - put - my - baggage - over - there?' My Captain made a gesture as though pouring from a jug, pointed to the Englishman, simulated the waving of a flag, then indicated the gentleman's shoes, saying 'Fill - your - British - boots!' Airports frequently display words in their own language next to the English equivalent. It often brought a smile to my face when approaching doors in Turkish airports, which are marked PUSH ITINIZ.

You will have experienced the passenger-handling side of an airport and probably be aware that there are facilities for handling mail and freight, including all forms of non-human animal life. In fact the only legal requirement for a field to become an aerodrome is the provision of a windsock! Modern airports need rather more than that, but you will always see one somewhere.

Runways are designated by their alignment in relation to Magnetic North to the nearest ten degrees. For example, a runway aligned north/south would be 36 (Three Six) or 18 (One Eight), depending on which way it was being used. As the Magnetic Pole (presently in north-eastern Canada) is moving, so the variation (the difference between true and magnetic north) changes. I can remember when I was a young Scout in North West London the variation being about 9°. Now it is less than 5°. Heathrow's two parallel runways started life as 28L (Two Eight Left) and 28R (Two

Eight Right). Some years ago their designation had to be changed to 27L and 27R because the variation had changed and it may not be many more years before they become 26L and 26R. These two runways are around 3750 metres (2¼ miles) long, allowing for very heavy take-offs. Initial departure routes are, as far as possible, over less noise-sensitive areas and monitoring posts are established to ensure they are complied with.

Substantial landing fees are charged, to cover the Customs and Ground Handling services provided. On short routes, such as London to Paris, these add disproportionately to an airline's costs and have to be reflected in the fares they charge.

As an aside, it is not well known that on the northern perimeter road at Heathrow there is an ancient cannon, marking one end of the baseline of the first accurate triangulation in England, which led to the formal founding of the Ordnance Survey. It was begun by General Roy in 1783, and the southern end of the base line (originally the corner of the workhouse at Hampton) some five miles across what was then Hounslow Heath, is also marked with a cannon in Roy Grove in the middle of a modern residential estate.

Airways and Navigation

One of the first things I was taught about night navigation was that, if I observed on the ground a red light with a white light underneath it, it was a brothel with the door open.

In the early days of airline flying, navigational corridors (airways) were set up on the busier routes across land, designated every hundred miles or so by radio beacons on the ground. Direction finders in the aircraft gave the crew the bearing of each transmitter and the simple task of 'beacon-crawling' along the designated route. These beacons, in the medium or long wave bands were subject to radio interference in stormy weather and 'coastal refraction' – bending of their beams as they passed from land to sea. There were crude area navigation aids, some based on systems devised for bombers in the Second World War. The beacons were improved and VHF transmitters installed, which, though of shorter range, gave generally accurate bearings, and ranges were also made available through Distance Measuring Equipment (DME).

These VORs (VHF Omni-directional Radio Ranges) can often be seen on airfields, and, if you know where to look, in open countryside under established airways. There are large numbers all over the World. One, for example, can be seen on the cliffs at Seaford Head marking the London to Paris route, and another about three miles north-east of Midhurst in West Sussex along the route to Southampton and Land's End. They are housed in small round buildings with a circular array of aerials. They work electronically, but the most understandable analogy is that of a lighthouse with a white beam rotating at a given speed, say, 360° in sixty seconds. If an observer saw a red light flash every time the white beam passed through

THE P2'S FLIGHT INSTRUMENT PANEL SHOWS ALL THE FLIGHT
INSTRUMENT FAIL FLAGS. THE INSTRUMENT COMPARATOR,
AFCS WARNING AND AFCS MODES INDICATORS DISPLAY THE
WORD LEGENDS THAT APPEAR WHEN THE RESPECTIVE TEST 2
SWITCH IS PRESSED.

Lockheed TriStar Co-Pilot Flight Instrument Panel

Magnetic North, he would only have to measure the elapsed time between that and seeing the white beam to know his bearing from the lighthouse. There are occasionally siting problems, which distort the signals, but generally VORs provide accurate navigational information at line-of-sight ranges (up to about 250 miles at aircraft cruising level). There are usually two VOR receivers in each aircraft. Presentation of their readings to the pilot is on two instruments, one a compass repeater with the 360° on a disc rotating against a lubber line indicating Magnetic North. Superimposed on this are two needles painted red and green, one for each receiver, pointing to where the ground station is relative to the aircraft, so that the pilot can see instantly the heading on to which to turn, should he wish to fly to the VOR, or read off a bearing, should he want a position line from it. By selecting a track to or from the VOR, the pilot can have, on another instrument, a fly left/fly right indication to maintain that track.

Airways are established across the World on busy routes. They are usually ten miles wide and designated by a colour and a number, e.g. Amber 1, Red 3, etc., and some extend for thousands of miles. Clearance to use them is requested using this nomenclature. Specially protected routes for royal flights are set up temporarily and designated 'Purple Airways'.

Over oceans and uninhabited areas of land, crews had to rely on the crude area navigation aids mentioned above, where available, and on celestial observations. A specialist navigator would take star shots with a sextant from the roof of the flight deck and plot them on a chart. All the calculations necessary would have to be done beforehand, because the aircraft was moving (even in those days) at quite a speed. In order to get a fix, two, or better three, readings would be taken from different stars and the position lines they gave transposed along the supposed track at the assumed ground speed to allow for the elapsed time between the first and last readings. This would ideally produce a small triangle called a 'cocked hat', the centre of which was assumed to be the aircraft's position. By joining the previous fix to this and projecting the line forward, say, six minutes (one tenth of the determined speed in knots or miles per hour), any necessary change of heading could be calculated and a revised ETA for the next reporting point determined. The navigators were never said to be lost, though they may have been 'temporarily unaware of their exact whereabouts'!

In the 1960s the radio navigation aids over the Bay of Biscay were rather limited. There was a reliable beacon on Jersey but the one at St. Nazaire, operated by the French Air Force, was shut down in the late afternoon, when they finished operations for the day. There were several very low range beacons in northern Spain, which were of limited use, but nothing else before a good one at Villa Formosa on the Spanish/Portuguese border. Unknown to a Viscount crew flying one evening en route to Lisbon, the strong north-westerly winds which had been forecast had backed to south-westerly and they were forty-six minutes late on ETA for Villa

Formosa! Not having much idea exactly where they were and half expecting Gibraltar to go past on the left-hand side, they were somewhat relieved when the beacon on the border suddenly came up pointing ahead of them.

A compass was the basic navigation instrument, and still is, for manoeuvring the aircraft after take-off and before landing. It was slow to settle after a turn and subject to inaccuracies caused by metal or electrical circuits near it. The first problem was alleviated by combining it with a gyroscope and the second by placing sensors out on a wing or back in the fuselage and relaying their readings to the Flight Deck. It was still subject to unreliability near the Magnetic Poles, and very large corrections had to be applied to obtain navigational information in relation to True North.

Then came the Moon probes, requiring top quality navigation in three dimensions. The Inertial Navigation System (INS) was born, and it was soon installed in civil aircraft. The basis of INS is a trio of gyroscopes, one for each dimension, providing a steady platform on the principal of a spinning top. When the gyros have spun up and before moving off the parking stand, the crew tell the INS, in terms of latitude and longitude, where it is to within about 100 metres. It is then able to sense every movement of the aircraft in three dimensions, compute them against time, and thus to know its position and its rate of change in any direction. This applies to taxiing on the ground as much as to flying at any speed.

An INS senses the precise track of the aircraft, and, if the True Air Speed is introduced from other instruments, it can instantly calculate the wind obtaining at the time. It does this about every half second and provides effectively a constant read-out for the crew. Up to nine 'waypoints' can be programmed into the computer by the pilots, to define the desired route, be it along established airways to radio beacons or between points defined by latitude and longitude. With the addition of a Flight Management System, standard routes with as many waypoints as required can be fed into the system automatically. If forecast en-route winds are inserted, uncannily accurate estimated times of arrival can be read out several hours in advance. The crew can at any time overrule the INS manually.

It is a simple matter to miss out a waypoint, if Air Traffic Control authorises a direct routing. In countries, such as the United States and Canada, where advanced Air Traffic Control computers are installed, very long direct routings along Great Circle tracks (see **Maps and Charts** on page 43) can often be approved, even as far as from coast to coast. Accurate navigation is possible over remote areas without ground radio aids, and flights in the Polar regions do not have to make allowances for poor compass readings. Without updating, an INS system is accurate to within a few hundred metres on a seven- or eight-hour flight. I once operated from Lisbon to Windhoek (Namibia) non-stop, about a seven-hour trip. None of the crew had been to Windhoek before. Its airport is not easily spotted in typical African bushland. We started our descent when the INS told us we were 140 miles out, and the INS led us right over the top of the control tower at 2000 feet above the field.

A turn downwind, parallel to the runway, followed a few seconds later by another of 180°, put us in a perfect position on final approach. Later versions of the INS have included constant updating by reference to Earth satellites. An instant read-out of present position with incredible accuracy, with track and distance to any programmed waypoint, is available.

Usually three INS sets are carried, two of them cross-checking each other and feeding into the autopilot for automatic navigation. The third one can be used as a monitor and also programmed individually with useful waypoints off the route. For example, on a transatlantic flight, the third INS is routinely programmed with the co-ordinates of Prestwick (Scotland), Gander (Newfoundland) and Keflavik (Iceland), or any other suitable airport, so that, at the flick of a switch, the crew can read the track and distance to any of them, in case of an in-flight emergency. In the latest aircraft, Global Positioning Systems are carried (using artificial satellites), which give an accurate position of the nose, let alone the rest of the plane! This information is passed to individual passenger seats via the in-flight entertainment equipment, so that you can follow the progress of the flight at all times.

Should Air Traffic Control require the aircraft to cross a point en route at a particular time and Flight Level, the necessary rate of climb and speed can be calculated by a computer and the appropriate power settings applied automatically.

The presence of other aircraft nearby can be detected by a Traffic Collision Avoidance System, which presents both their position and Flight Level.

Altimeters

Because of the long history of American and British aviation, most altimeters read in feet. One thousand feet is a convenient unit for such things as vertical separation between aircraft and terrain clearance; its equivalent in metres (say, 300) and multiples thereof are not quite so comfortable to use. Altimeters, like barometers, measure the pressure of the atmosphere above them by the expansion or contraction of a small evacuated capsule. The movement is minuscule but is translated to the needles of the altimeter 'by a suitable system of levers' (somewhat of an understatement!). Covering from sea level to 40,000 feet requires the large needle to go round the dial forty times. These movements are often supplemented electronically to provide a digital presentation, which is much less subject to misreading.

Atmospheric pressure varies from hour to hour and place to place. Altimeter pressure settings can be adjusted on a subscale, so that the instrument reads height (the vertical distance between the aircraft and a particular spot on the ground, such as an airfield) or altitude (the elevation above sea level). For want of anything better, these settings are referred to by three-letter cyphers dating from the 1930s when Morse code was used for ground-to-air communication, as the QFE and the QNH respectively.

At lower levels, altimeters are set to the local QNH, which, as it varies from place to place, has to be reset regularly as the aircraft progresses along its route. Vertical separation between aircraft on different headings is at least 500 feet and levels are dictated by the compass sector in which their track lies. When clear of terrain, all aircraft set their altimeters on a standard setting of 1013·2 millibars, derived from the average surface air pressure around the World. This means that vertical separation standards are constant and reliable. Altimeter readings are then called Flight Levels. Below 29,000 feet (referred to as Flight Level Two Nine Zero), 1,000 feet between aircraft is perfectly adequate. Above that level the separation is increased to 2,000 feet, to allow for possible inaccuracies of altimeters. Most jet airliners operate at the latter heights. Cruising Flight Levels on tracks between North and South through East are 290, 330, 370 and 410, and those between South and North through West are 310, 350 and 390. Over the southern United Kingdom, reduced vertical separation has been introduced in order to provide for heavier traffic flows. This has recently been extended to other busy areas of Europe. It is deemed acceptable because of improved altimeter reliability.

A notable exception to these rules is on routes across the North Atlantic, which are clearly defined and provide guaranteed lateral separation. This is necessary because of the uneven flow of traffic. For commercial reasons most airlines leave Europe in the mid- to late morning, so that arrival in the United States or Canada, allowing for the time-zone change, is only an hour or two after departure. This leads to a heavy demand for airspace by predominantly westbound aircraft in the morning. Likewise, there is strong pressure on available routes and flight levels overnight, because aircraft set out eastwards in the evening and arrive in the early morning, having lost five or so hours of local time en route while the passengers try to sleep.

In earlier times, when unpressurised aircraft were restricted to altitudes of 10,000 feet or below, a well-known phenomenon applicable to polar regions was the fact that altimeters could overread by as much as 4,000 feet. If, for a given column of air, much of it is very cold and therefore dense, the majority sinks to a low level. So the altimeter senses less weight of air above itself and indicates that it is much higher than it really is. Several mountains in Greenland exceed 8,000 feet in height, so great care had to be taken to ensure adequate terrain clearance.

Climatology

One of the first things a pilot has to learn is the difference between weather and climate. Weather is if it is raining or snowing; climate is the best thing you can do with a ladder.

Climatology is a most interesting subject. A lot of British holiday makers seem to be under the impression that once you are past Dover, it is always sunny! It certainly pays to make a few enquiries about weather conditions in other parts of the

World. I can recommend *The World Weather Guide* by E. A. Pearce and C. G. Smith (Helicon, Oxford). I was once told by a friend that he had been offered a cheap holiday in Cyprus in February. I advised him that I was not surprised. If he wanted to see horizontal rain, Cyprus in February was a good place to go! Any other time of the year in Cyprus can be a delight.

It is pretty obvious that you don't go to India in July or August. Other countries have monsoons as well, and it's a good idea to find out when. Thailand has three seasons instead of four. The cool season, November to March, is when the temperature only reaches 33° Celsius in the early afternoon. It is followed by the hot season and the rainy season.

Summer in Hong Kong is hot and wet, and occasional typhoons cause structural damage and loss of life between July and September. Other places with interesting local winds are Nice and Marseilles, where the bitterly cold Mistral (named after a local poet) is generated by dense, low-temperature air collecting over the Alps and roaring down the Rhône Valley for a few days in spring.

The Adriatic coast of the former Yugoslavia has warm, sunny summers and mild winters, but occasionally these are interrupted for a few days by the Bora, a cold wind from central and eastern Europe similar to the Mistral.

Egypt from March to early June can have its normally fine, sunny weather marred by the most unpleasant Khamsin, a hot, dust-laden wind from the desert, raising sand particles which seriously reduce visibility and irritate eyes, nose and mouth.

Tropical regions are subject to rainy seasons a month or two after the apparent passage of the Sun overhead. Nairobi, close to the Equator, has a weak one in April and May, and another in November, but Mexico City, not far south of the Tropic of Cancer, has quite heavy rains from June to September.

Condensation Trails (Contrails)

You will probably not be able to see condensation trails streaming behind the engines, even if you are sitting in the rear of the aircraft, because they form some way back. You will, of course, have seen them behind high-flying aircraft from the ground. When fuel is burned, a very small amount of water is released. Because the temperature of the air is so low (say, minus 50° C at 33,000 feet) even this is enough to saturate the air and the water condenses into cloud. The contrails may persist or dissipate quickly, depending on atmospheric conditions, or may be blown out of line by high winds.

En route weather

Stratified cloud will normally generate very slight turbulence, if any at all, but thunderstorms are a different matter. The clouds associated with them are called cumulonimbus (sometimes shortened to cunim or Cb), from the Latin words for 'to heap up' and 'rain'. Inside such clouds there are strong up-currents and down-currents (there is no such thing as an airpocket!), which make flight in them very uncomfortable. There is an outside chance of a lightning strike (I have only experienced four or five in thirty-seven years of flying), which, with a little exaggeration, could be something on which to dine out! Actually, little harm will come to the aircraft, as it is electrically bonded – possibly a very small hole in a wing where the strike actually occurs and a slight chance of affecting one of the compasses. Most radio aerials are now enclosed in the fuselage and so are not vulnerable.

Due to surface tension, the water droplets in the cloud can be in liquid form with their temperature below freezing (supercooled). As the aircraft passes through them, the tension is broken and ice forms instantly, in the same way as freezing rain glazes over a road. This could, of course, be a serious hazard, but de-icing equipment is more than adequate. Hot air from the engine compressors is ducted along the leading edge of the wings, melting the ice practically before it forms. There is a risk of damage by hail to the nose and leading edges of the wings. Unless the hailstones are particularly large, this is only likely to strip off some of the paint.

If the edges of a thunderhead are sharply defined, the cloud consists of water droplets, even though the temperature may be below freezing. The droplets are 'supercooled'. If the cloud appears wispy, they have turned to ice crystals.

There have been reports of spectacular fireballs rolling down an aircraft's aisle, but these are rare. One very beautiful phenomenon seen at night on the Flight Deck windows when flying in areas of high static electricity is St. Elmo's Fire. Described in the days of sailing ships as running up the masts, the fascinating blue discharges of static make a wonderful sight, looking like miniature lightning strikes but lasting long enough to be seen clearly.

In any case, for your comfort your pilot will avoid flying into thunderstorms whenever possible. He may not be able to avoid them when descending into a terminal zone or approaching to land. The aircraft are equipped with weather radar, the beams from which reflect off rain, which is present in large amounts in cumulonimbus clouds. He will be able easily to see where the cores are and fly round them. However, if you are flying in tropical regions, you may encounter the Intertropical Convergence Zone. This is the region which migrates north and south seasonally with the apparent movement of the Sun, where the heat causes rising air and the trade winds are drawn in to replace it. The Zone's position varies according to whether it is over a continent or an ocean, but in any case it generates an almost unbroken line of thunderstorms around 100 miles deep. Your pilot will do his best to pick a way through them, and the consequent turbulence should only last ten to fifteen minutes. At night the zone provides a spectacular display of almost continuous lightning flashes.

Observation of a well-developed thunderstorm from a distance provides more than passing interest. An 'unstable' atmosphere, is one in which the temperature

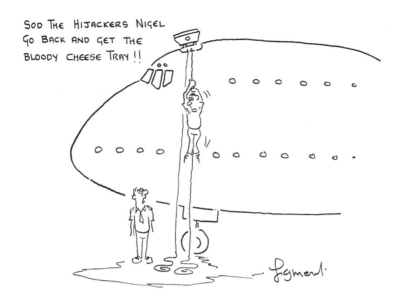

SOD THE HIJACKERS NIGEL
GO BACK AND GET THE
BLOODY CHEESE TRAY !!

decreases with height at a faster rate than rising air. This means that, once triggered off, a pocket of warm air in such a region will always be at a higher temperature than its surroundings. It will therefore continue to rise and will carry on doing so until it reaches the tropopause, the level in the Earth's atmosphere at which temperature ceases to decrease with altitude. The tops of thunderstorms flatten out and spread downwind, assuming a typical 'anvil' shape. The tropopause varies in height with the seasons and with latitude, being as low as 26,000 feet over the Poles and up to 58,000 feet in the Tropics. Hence tropical thunderstorms can reach heights unattainable by conventional aircraft, which have to try to fly round them. In temperate zones however, where the triggering temperatures are lower, it is usually possible to climb high enough to top the anvil clouds. At night you might be lucky enough to see the rare phenomenon of lightning discharging upwards into clear air.

An interesting occurrence you may occasionally see, even from the ground in Britain, is rain falling from a thundercloud but evaporating before it reaches the ground. This is called virga (from the Latin for a rod).

The wind varies considerably from the surface of the Earth upwards. In free air, say above 2,000 feet, it circulates anti-clockwise around an area of low pressure in the Northern Hemisphere and the other way round in the Southern. (It is for the same reason that your bathwater goes down the plug-hole the opposite way in the Southern Hemisphere!) Winds should flow directly from high pressure to low, but are deflected by the rotation of the Earth and actually blow parallel to the isobars (lines joining points of equal atmospheric pressure). Because of surface friction,

38

wind close to the ground is deflected slightly less and the air flows inwards at about 30° to the isobars. Pressure patterns at altitude can be quite different from those at the surface, so the winds are too. Especially in the winter months, narrow streams of very high-speed wind form. These are called 'jetstreams' and wind speeds in excess of 150 miles per hour are common. Flying in them can be quite smooth, but on the edges, where the speed is changing rapidly, severe turbulence can be present in clear air. These areas are impossible to see and do not show up on radar, because there is nothing to reflect the beam. Fortunately the forecasters can give the pilots a very good idea of their location, and it may be possible to avoid them by selecting a different route or a lower or higher cruising level. The Captain's room for manoeuvre may, however, be limited by the presence of other aircraft or a limitation on routes available. Clear air turbulence occurs quite frequently over the Maritime Provinces of Canada, where there is often a kink in the alignment of the jetstreams. Regular transatlantic travellers may well have experienced it – about two hours after take-off from New York, just as drinks are being served!

In temperate latitudes, winds aloft are predominantly westerly, which is why it takes at least an hour longer to cross the Atlantic westbound than the other way. Westerly upper winds move southwards with the Sun, so that schedules across India are changed in winter. As the winds do not conveniently alter precisely on the date the airlines change their schedules, in the autumn you can arrive an hour late eastbound (and in the spring an hour early), because the new season's winds have not set in.

Not many people know of the story of Dimitri, a poor little Greek lad who came to London in search of work. He looked around for some time to find somewhere to live and eventually climbed to the roof of a new high-rise building under construction. Here he found a contractor's hut, which was ideal, and he made his home in it.

When the building was completed, it was occupied by the Weather Bureau, and the girls from the top floor used to come out on to the roof every half-hour to take readings of temperature, rainfall and wind velocity. They got very friendly with Dimitri and he looked forward to chatting with them. When the winter set in, the girls did not fancy leaving their warm office and going up on to the cold roof, so they persuaded Dimitri to take the readings for them, write them on a piece of paper and dangle them down to the office window.

This arrangement went very well at first, but one morning (after the night before?) Dimitri made a complete mess of it, and what he wrote on the paper was totally illogical. That was how it became known as Dimitri Illogical Office.

Engines

Four-stroke piston engines have a 'suck, squeeze, bang, blow' sequence. That is, the fuel/air mixture is sucked into the cylinders, compressed, ignited and exhausted. Jet engines have a similar cycle, except that the whole flow is smooth and uninterrupted by the reciprocation of pistons, hence saving a huge amount of wear and tear and being a great deal more efficient. The thrust produced by each of the three RB 211s on a TriStar is equivalent to that of twenty-one of the Rolls Royce Merlins fitted to a Spitfire, the most powerful engines of their time. Bigger, better and more economical aircraft have developed throughout the history of aviation as more power has become available.

Air is taken in through a large compressor, some six to seven feet in diameter. It is compressed through several stages and passed into the combustion chambers where there are five to seven oversize blowlamps. These heat the compressed air with core temperatures reaching 1100° C. It then passes across several stages of turbine, which are connected via concentric shafts to power the compressors. The remainder flows out of the jet pipe rather quickly, generating a huge amount of thrust. In by-pass engines, favoured by most aircraft manufacturers, a large proportion of the compressed air does not enter the combustion chambers, but by-passes them, being added to the jet efflux, in fact generating some 70% of the total thrust. Thus, the compressor blades act as very efficient ducted propellers. The whole engine is quieter and the noise generated is of a much more acceptable pitch.

When the engines are shut down on the ground, they idle over, especially in strong winds, showing how freely they rotate. You may hear quite a loud clattering noise from them. This is perfectly normal and derives from the mounting of the individual compressor blades on their driveshaft. This is usually in the form of a 'Christmas tree' joint. When the engine is spooled up, the blades are thrown outwards by centrifugal force and held tight in their mountings.

Running jet engines, even at idle power, should never be approached from the front or the rear. Describing the efflux as a red-hot gale would be an understatement. Through the front, the engine draws in the air volume of a large room every second, so it should be given a very wide berth.

Flight Instruments

One of the first things a pilot has to learn is that, when flying blind, he must believe what his instruments tell him, in spite of physical indications to the contrary. The forces in an aircraft give completely different sensations in the balance system of the inner ear and it can feel as though you are turning left, when in fact you are flying straight and level, or rolling to the right. We are all used to experiencing a sense of balance when standing on the ground, even when we are blindfolded. When flying in cloud, we have neither the reaction from our feet nor visual clues.

The conventional layout of instruments in front of the Captain (who always sits in the left-hand seat, except in helicopters) is, in the centre, an artificial horizon (a gimballed gyroscope which shows the aircraft's attitude in pitch and roll) above a compass (usually gyro-enhanced). To the upper left is the airspeed indicator (reading in knots – see **Navigation**); this usually has a machmeter built into it (measuring the aircraft's speed as a decimal of the local speed of sound – it is the compressibility effects of the air in which we are really interested. The speed of sound is merely a convenient way to refer to the speed of pressure waves through a fluid). Underneath it is a repeat of the compass with direction finder needles superimposed. These can be tuned to radio beacons on the ground. To the right are an altimeter and a vertical speed indicator (showing rate of climb or descent). There is a cunning device with three needles, the thinnest of which takes exactly one minute to complete a circuit of its dial while the others measure how many times this has happened. This is called a clock.

These instruments are repeated in front of the right-hand seat for the First Officer, who is thus able to monitor the progress of the aircraft or fly it himself (see page 31). In the centre are several instruments for each engine – the more you have, the more you know about what is going on. Modern engine instruments are of the vertical strip type, so it is easy to see, if they are all aligned, that all the engines are performing similarly. Between the seats is a pedestal housing autopilot and engine controls, including throttles (thrust 'levvers' (sic) in American parlance!). There are panels above the front Flight Deck windows and another in the roof, with circuit breakers and switches. The size of the Flight Deck has to be limited so that all these controls are accessible to the pilots while they are strapped in their seats. It was the height of luxury on the Lockheed L-1011 TriStar to have room to put down a briefcase between the pilot's seat and the outer wall.

To monitor the hydraulic, electrical, air conditioning, pressurisation systems and much else there used to be a Flight Engineer's station with a large panel down the right hand wall behind the First Officer but visible from the Captain's seat. With the advent of cathode ray tube presentations (the 'glass cockpit'), it has been possible to do away with both the Flight Engineer and his panel, and reduce the operating crew to just the two pilots. In the Boeing 747-400, for example, over 1000 instruments and switches have been reduced to 300 and many of the systems automated. A Central Warning System, plus individual lights or aural indications, draw the pilots' attention immediately to any malfunction.

Flight Recorders and Cockpit Voice Recorders

Flight Recorders are what the press insists on calling 'black boxes' – they are in fact painted bright orange. They record on wire a large number of parameters, so that they are invaluable not only for accident investigation but for performance monitoring of the aircraft. Providing the pilot has done his job properly, he has nothing to fear, and in fact they can provide evidence on his side in the event of an investigation into an incident. Cockpit Voice Recorders, which also pick up Flight Deck aural warnings, only run for half an hour before recycling and are automatically wiped at the end of an uneventful flight, preserving the privacy and the confidence of the Flight Deck crews. Should a Captain wish to preserve a recording of an event more than half an hour before landing, he is able to do so.

Flying controls

The ailerons are hinged flaps on the outer trailing edge of the wings. When the control column is moved to the left, the right aileron goes down, increasing the lift on the right wing; the left aileron goes up, resulting in the opposite effect, so the aircraft banks to the left. Some of the lift from the wings then acts towards the left and a turn in that direction is initiated. If the control column were held in the same position, the left wing would continue to drop until the aircraft turned upside down, so it has to be returned to its neutral point, but the bank remains and the turn continues. This is the opposite to what happens when a car is steered into a turn; if the steering wheel is returned to neutral, the vehicle, of course, straightens up.

The elevators are hinged flaps mounted on the tailplane (the small horizontal 'wings' at the rear). When the control column is moved to the rear the elevators rise, generating a downward pressure on the tailplane, and, being attached to it by the fuselage, the nose rises. The opposite occurs when the pilot wants to drop the nose. In some aircraft the whole tailplane moves.

The rudder is a hinged flap attached to the fin (the vertical structure at the back of the fuselage). This is used to control any side-to-side movement (yaw) during take-off and landing, and to keep the aircraft straight in the event of uneven power being applied to a multi-engined machine.

Because these controls have to operate over a wide range of speeds and the back-pressure at the top of the range would be too much for the pilot, they are assisted by hydraulic rams. In fact the input from the flying controls in the Flight Deck is simply to one side of a hydraulic system. Because the pilot could otherwise unknowingly apply too harsh a control input, possibly causing structural damage, artificial 'feel' is built into the system using springs. There are multiple separate hydraulic systems operating discrete sections of all the flying controls, so that a failure of one, two, or even three hydraulic systems would still leave the aircraft controllable, as would external damage to part of an aileron, elevator or rudder.

The cable input from the Captain's controls to the hydraulics follows a separate path from that of the First Officer's. The two are connected in two places, under the Flight Deck and near the hydraulic jacks, so that the controls move together, but, in the event of a cable jam, they can be separated and the Captain can fly the aircraft through the First Officer's path and vice versa. The cables are so strong that both pilots pulling together with all their strength could not possibly break them.

Maps and charts

The main problem with making a map of the Earth is that the relationship to each other of points on a curved surface has to be portrayed on a flat piece of paper. This

42

means that there is bound to be distortion on some part of it. Where this distortion is depends on the type of projection. The map of the World with which we are probably most familiar is drawn on a Mercator projection. Gerhardus Mercator was the Latinised name of Gerhard Kremer, a sixteenth-century Flemish cartographer and mathematician. He drew the lines of latitude and longitude at right angles to each other. This makes the construction of the grid very simple, but it means that, while tropical regions are fairly accurately portrayed, there is great distortion near the Poles. Greenland is actually only three times the size of the island of Borneo, which lies on the Equator, but on a Mercator projection it appears to have at least fifteen times the area.

A considerable advantage of the Mercator projection is that a straight line joining two points crosses each line of longitude at the same angle, meaning that a course set by an aircraft (discounting allowances for a change of wind en route) would be constant from departure to destination. However, this straight line is not the shortest distance over a curved surface. On a short flight this makes little difference, but on a longer one it is highly significant. The shortest distance is actually along a curve, called a Great Circle, whose plane passes through the centre of the Earth. On the face of it, one might expect that a flight between London and New York would route out over Land's End and make its first landfall near Nantucket six hours later. In fact you are more likely to spend the first hour and a half flying up to Glasgow and out over the Western Isles. You will then be over the Atlantic Ocean for only three hours before reaching the Canadian coast over Newfoundland. The rest of the flight is over land, following the coast, which runs southwards and westwards to New York and beyond. Only about half of the flight is over water, the route being close to the Great Circle, which forms a broad curve towards the North Pole. A closer look at a map might produce the surprise that most of Newfoundland is south of the English Channel, yet you are likely to see icebergs in the area, even in summer. This is because of the effect on the climate of the huge American continent to the west and the cold northerly sea currents in which fish abound, which made Boston the biggest fishing port in the World. New York is on about the same latitude as Madrid, yet has bitterly cold winters (and hot summers), because it enjoys (?) an east-coast continental climate.

On flights to points in the United States which are farther to the west, the route takes you even more to the north. You will fly across Iceland and at least the middle of Greenland (a spectacular sight), then on via the vast, practically-uninhabited expanse of northern Canada, a beautiful land of snow and lakes as far as the eye can see. The Sun appears to go round the Equator at about 1,040 miles per hour. It is perhaps interesting to note that an airliner flying at 550 mph in latitudes in excess of 60° is circumnavigating the Earth faster than the apparent passage of the Sun (the cosine of 60° being 0·5). At the right time of the day you can even observe the Sun rising in the west!

Another surprise generated by our familiarity with the World as depicted by Mercator is that, were an aircraft capable of flying non-stop for twenty hours, plus reserves, and were it commercially viable, the shortest route from London to Auckland, New Zealand (longitude $174^1/_2°$ East), would pass very close to the North Pole. We are so used to the idea that New Zealand is south-east of England that the concept of setting off due north seems quite peculiar!

One big advantage of having latitude shown on a map is that you immediately have a scale. By definition, one degree of latitude is 60 nautical miles. A nautical mile is 6,080 feet, just a little over 15% more than a statute mile of 5,280 feet, which was originally the distance a Roman soldier would march in 1,000 paces. The kilometre, established under Napoleon, is a much more scientific measure, being one forty-thousandth of the circumference of the World (roughly five-eighths of a statute mile). Because the distance and track between two points defined by latitude and longitude can easily be calculated by geometry and trigonometry, the nautical mile is used for both air and maritime navigation. Speeds are expressed in knots (nautical miles per hour). Thus expressions such as 'a rate of knots' or 'knots per hour' are tautological nonsense.

Projections other than Mercator's are used for maps, depending on their purpose. For flights in polar regions, a projection made as though you were looking vertically down on the Pole can be useful, though the map becomes progressively more distorted with distance from the centre. The Conical Orthomorphic (true shape) projection is often found in atlases. It is translated as though a cone of paper sits on the curved surface, touching it as a tangent. Again, distortion increases with distance from the supposed point of contact. British Ordnance Survey maps are aligned with the National Grid. Latitude and longitude are also featured and the small variation between the two grids can be seen. It is of minor consequence over small areas.

Medical factors

When we breathe in, the atmospheric pressure forces the oxygen in the air through the thin-walled blood vessels in our lungs (the bronchioles) and into our blood for distribution to the main organs and round our bodies. If we climb up a mountain, the proportion of oxygen in the air by volume remains constant, but the pressure decreases and we start to have difficulty in absorbing enough oxygen. This is usually no problem until we climb higher than 10,000 feet, but reaching the top of Mount Everest without taking in extra oxygen is almost a superhuman feat.

Because jet aircraft are only efficient at levels around 30,000 feet and above, we need to pressurise the cabin, so that passengers and crew can breathe normally. As the difference in pressure between sea level and these altitudes is so great, it would be impractical to build an aircraft strong enough, but at a realistic weight, to achieve a really low cabin altitude. It would probably be impossible to provide windows, for example. So a compromise is reached. With a pressure differential between the inside and outside of about eight pounds per square inch, the cabin altitude is about 6,000 feet, while the aircraft is at, say, 33,000 feet. The rate of change of cabin altitude in the climb or descent can be kept to about 300 feet per minute, normally undetectable by the passengers or crew. Doors are designed as a plug fit, opening inwards, so that it would be quite impossible to open them against even a fraction of the pressure.

At 6,000 feet there is a slight reduction in the amount of oxygen our lungs take in. This does no harm over a few hours, especially as we are sitting still most of the time, and our bodies quickly recover after landing. It does explain, however, the increasingly adverse effect of alcohol, which though it is for most people enjoyable, should be taken only in moderation. Very unpleasant hangovers can result from over-indulgence in the air (and before departure)!

In the extremely unlikely situation of a failure in the cabin pressurisation system, an oxygen mask for every seat drops out of the roof, hanging in front of you by its supply tube. This is known in the trade as the 'rubber jungle'. You can imagine how long it takes to restow all the masks, if their deployment has been caused by a faulty signal to the switch! If you do need to use them look after yourself first, before attending to children or others. You will be no use to anyone if you are affected by anoxia yourself. You will know if the emergency is for real. You will feel a popping sensation in your ears and mist will form in the cabin. The engine noise will decrease, as the Captain initiates a rapid descent to a lower altitude. No one should suffer any significant trauma, but it would be prudent to have a check-up at an early stage.

We breathe in and out about a litre of air seven times a minute. Multiply this by four hundred people and you will understand why the cabin air has to be changed every two and a half to three minutes. This is achieved by taking compressed air off the engines, cooling it and ducting it through the cabin and the freight holds (in case live animals are being transported) in a continuous flow. Cabin air pressure is controlled automatically by discharge valves. As the air originates from outside, it is very dry. To humidify it adequately would require the aircraft to carry more water than fuel, which is obviously totally impracticable. The situation is aggravated by tobacco smoke and this is one reason why smoking has been banned on many flights.

Typical humidities in the cabin can be 20% or lower, compared with perhaps 80% on the ground, and our bodies dry out quickly. We perspire, but are unaware of it because the sweat evaporates as soon as it reaches the surface of our skin. A lot of moisture is lost. In extreme cases, humidities as low as 8% have been measured and prolonged exposure at these levels without liquid intake can lead to re-absorption of our own urine and kidney damage. The cabin crew simply do not have enough time to come round with drinks for everyone more than, say, once an hour. The consumption of alcohol accelerates dehydration and so, to some extent, do coffee and tea. Drinking water is available, usually outside the toilets, but it is often not convenient to leave your seat frequently to get it. So I suggest that you carry on board with you a bottle of mineral water. You have to be cautious even with this, because some spa waters have a high salt content and are therefore self-defeating as far as quenching thirst is concerned. If possible, take a small intake of water every fifteen minutes or so. It is well worthwhile to take a shower or bath at the earliest opportunity after landing. You will be substantially refreshed.

Some years ago, I was faced with a real humdinger of a problem on a long-range TriStar. The domestic water supply is pumped from a reservoir round the aircraft to the various outlets in galleys, toilets, etc. When the system is replenished, the pressure is released before the tank can be refilled. Afterwards the inflow valve has to be closed and sealed, or the system will not repressurise. We had taken off from Bombay (now Mumbai) for a 9½-hour night flight to London, and the Cabin Services Director reported to me that there was no fresh water supply throughout the aircraft. It sometimes took a little while for the system to repressurise, but it soon became clear that this was not going to happen. We had no potable water, so could not make tea or coffee and the only drinkable liquid we had on board was the contents of about two small cans of 'mixers' for each of our 200 or so passengers – clearly nowhere near enough for a long flight, without risking kidney damage.

Without dumping fuel, we would not be down to our maximum landing weight until we reached Ankara, about five hours' flying ahead. There were no British Airways staff at Ankara at that time, and the prospect of arriving in the early hours of the morning and asking for 300 bottles of mineral water did not seem very promising! A return to Bombay after dumping about 10,000 gallons of fuel overboard or a landing at Teheran (the first available airport en route) were not attractive propositions. The first would almost certainly have resulted in a very extensive delay, because the long single-sector night duty would turn into a two-sector one and we would be setting off at least three hours into our legally permitted duty time. The remainder would not have been sufficient for us to fly all the way to London and a replacement crew would have had to be positioned to somewhere like Istanbul or perhaps Munich, with an inevitable delay while they were called up from home and flown there. Another complete crew was not available at Bombay, and if we were to stay with the flight, we would have been required to take a twelve-hour rest period before proceeding. A stop in Teheran would also have required the dumping of a substantial amount of fuel and we would still have run up against a Flight Time Limitations problem.

It is in this sort of situation that a Flight Engineer comes into his own, with his intimate knowledge of the aircraft's design. I was fortunate to have a very talented young one that night. He reasoned that the problem was caused by the

AND THE FINAL TEST REQUIRES THE CANDIDATE TO DRINK THREE PINTS OF BEER AND [CENSORED] ON A SHILLING FROM FIVE PACES!!

M.C.P. AIRWAYS
PILOT
SELECTION.
INTERVIEWS
ISOMETRIC TESTS
APTITUDE TESTS

Pigment

replenishment valve not having been properly closed and sealed. On the TriStar 1, there are two lifts which are used for access to a food-preparation galley under the passenger cabin, and from this it is possible to go through bulkheads, via the Electrical Equipment Bay, and into the Forward Freight Hold, which is normally filled with pallets. The cable control for the valve in question is accessible from inside the aircraft as well as from the outside. Things were different on the long-range TriStar 500 (which we called the 'sports-car version'). The fuselage was shorter and the passenger capacity lower. The downstairs galley was replaced by extra fuel tanks. Access to the Electrical Equipment Bay was through a small hole in the floor of the passenger cabin. Climbing down through this, my Flight Engineer was able to squeeze through into the forward freight hold and, being slim, could just ease his way past the pallets stowed there. Unfortunately the 500 series does not have access to the water valve cable from inside the aircraft, but, knowing exactly where it was, my Flight Engineer, with a large screwdriver destroyed part of the interior panelling on this sparkling new aircraft (which had been delivered only one week before). He was able to reach through the hole, grasp the cable and seal the pumping circuit, restoring the aircraft's water supply. He probably saved the company several years' worth of his salary that night, and avoided a serious disruption to the journey of a large number of passengers.

If our skulls were solid, they would be so heavy that our neck muscles would not be able to hold them upright. To make them lighter, there are large holes, called sinuses (from the Latin for a 'pocket'), which are lined with mucus. If we have a cold or other nasal infection, the mucus becomes swollen. Air can pass out of the passages but not easily back in. As the cabin altitude increases, the falling air pressure equalises between the interior and exterior of the sinuses without our noticing. However, during the descent, when the pressure is increasing, the low pressure inside the sinuses tends to remain there and the difference with the outside causes discomfort and, in some cases, pain, which may become severe. Unless there is a major fault in the pressurisation control, we will at most feel a minor blocking sensation in our ears, which are separated from the nasal passages only by our eardrums. Normally the simple expedient of pinching our noses and blowing gently will clear the sinuses.

In order to keep fit, one pilot installed parallel bars in his home. The effort it took to get a drink from both of them at the same time ....

Weather limits for landing

Landings, and take-offs, are normally made into wind, to reduce the length of runway required. However, surrounding terrain, as at Mauritius, Dalaman (Southern Turkey), Salonika and a number of other airports dictate that landings and take-offs are made in opposite directions (towards and away from high ground). It may be, therefore, that only a light wind is too strong, if it is blowing from the wrong quarter. As far as crosswinds are concerned, large aircraft can cope with about 40 knots (a full gale) at right angles to the runway, with gusts up to 55 or 60 knots. There are one or two airports where terrain or hangars close to the runway cause undue turbulence or downdraughts, and wind limits for landing are reduced accordingly. A vertical sea wall below the runway at Heraklion, Crete, can cause a few problems with a strong northerly wind.

In the event of unserviceability or non-provision of precision aids, weather limits are raised to suit. A number of holiday destinations in less well-developed countries and probably with sea and mountains near their airports may have very limited approach aids, in which case very high weather limits apply. However, it is the knowledge that the weather there is expected to be good that makes the passengers want to go these places, so there is usually little disruption to services. For example, landing at Corfu requires five miles visibility, because of an oblique approach path and the proximity of high ground, but the number of occasions when less than that obtains is very small indeed. With precision approach aids, typical limits for a manual landing are 600 metres runway visual range and a 200-foot cloud base. See **Chapter 5** for automatic landings.

3

Pre-flight Planning and Checks

A crew reports for duty at least an hour before scheduled departure time. The Cabin Crew are thoroughly briefed as to their particular part in the team by the senior member, even though they are familiar with their duties. They also run through emergency procedures as a matter of routine. None of them assumes this is unnecessary even though they have done it countless times before. Practice makes perfect!

The Captain and his First Officer report to a Duty Officer, who advises them of the names of the other crew members, the stand on which their aircraft is parked and any VIPs expected on the flight. This may affect security arrangements. The two pilots assess the meteorological situation, looking at the weather at the departure and destination airfields, plus alternates in the event of having to make a diversion. They are also interested in the en route weather at their expected cruising level and conditions at airports along the way. Forecasts and hourly actual reports are available, as are satellite photographs which help to pinpoint the position of weather systems and fronts. The pilots look at details, provided by the Flight Information Service, of the serviceability of runways, lighting and radio aids, together with restrictions applied for political reasons, or for royal or VIP flights. On the basis of this and in consultation with the Dispatcher who has details of the commercial load, the Captain, and only the Captain, decides how much fuel he requires.

A Boeing 747 uses around 3,000 imperial gallons (13,200 litres) per hour in the cruise, a little over 300 yards to the gallon. This may seem a rather high consumption, but is in fact roughly the same amount of fuel that would be required to move 400 passengers in 100 cars at a fraction of the speed. A basic fuel requirement is usually worked out for the Captain by computer, the forecast en route winds having been entered, and he uses this for guidance. The amount of fuel he takes is entirely his decision and may involve offloading freight or passengers in extreme cases, for example if the weather at destination is likely to be close to his operating limits and his diversion fields are distant. Within Europe and the United States, where there are hundreds of suitable airports, this is rarely a problem, but further afield it may become critical. Alternates for Mumbai (Bombay), for example, are Delhi or Chennai (Madras), both at least an hour and a half away. Ahmedabad is somewhat nearer, but might not have the best ground-handling facilities. There are no other airports in-between with runways long or strong enough to take a large airliner.

Local knowledge is vital in a case like this – Mumbai Airport is surrounded by housing that might be described by an estate agent as 'providing scope for the handyman'. Just after dawn, the residents start cooking their breakfast on open fires, burning fuel whose origin is not discussed in polite circles. There is a rapid increase in the smoke content of the air and the visibility can drop to below visual landing limits. If the flight is scheduled in at dawn, it might be prudent to have a little extra fuel to be able to wait until after breakfast. However, the flight from London is a ten-hour one and the aircraft is likely to burn about 7% per hour of any extra fuel, just to carry the increased weight, so starting off with an extra tonne of fuel only results in having 300 kg to use at the far end.

A commercial consideration on shorter sectors is the price of fuel at the destination. Jet aircraft burn kerosene (similar to paraffin), which is supplied to London Heathrow and Gatwick by pipeline from the refinery and so is relatively cheap. Where it has to be carried a long way by road or rail it can be very expensive and worth taking some or all of the return sector requirement on the outbound sector. Examples of this might be Milan or Warsaw.

The legal minimum fuel that a Captain is required to carry is that needed for the flight from departure to destination, plus 5% for navigational contingencies (rerouting to avoid thunderstorms, being restricted to a lower cruising level than planned because of other traffic, etc.). He must add to that enough to climb away from a missed approach and divert to a suitable alternate airfield, plus thirty minutes' holding when he gets there. He must use his judgement to decide whether this is enough and many will take a small extra amount for contingencies (usually referred to by the pilots as 'for the wife and kids'), but there is little point in carrying extra fuel without a specific idea of what it might be used for.

I spent some time flying an early version of the Boeing 707 on charter work, some of which was to the western seaboard of the United States. Bangor, in Maine, is just about half way from London to Los Angeles and made an excellent technical stop. It had superb ground handling, achieved offloading of all the passengers' luggage, clearance of US Customs and Immigration (a requirement at the first port of call), reloading, refuelling, recatering and a crew change, all in 45 minutes. Passengers could then leave Los Angeles Airport on arrival through a domestic terminal, saving any time they had lost en route. When a longer range 707 capable of flying non-stop became available, we found that it used so much fuel in the first half of the flight to Los Angeles in order to carry enough for the second half, that it was only marginally advantageous to operate it straight through.

It may come as a surprise that the payload of a large airliner is only a small part of its overall weight. The fuel is the heaviest single item. The Boeing 707, introduced in the 1960s, was the first aircraft able to lift more in fuel than its basic empty weight. Average passenger weight, including baggage, is taken as 80kg (176lbs or 12½ stone), so even 400 passengers on a Boeing 747 are only equivalent to the weight of fuel required for just over three hours' flying in the cruise. The fuel load is thus usually far greater than the weight of passengers, freight and mail that the aircraft can carry.

There are three weight limitations which directly affect the operation of the aircraft, the maxima for taxiing, taking-off and landing. Usually about 200 gallons (900 litres) are burned between the aircraft leaving the stand and reaching the end of the take-off runway. The maximum taxi weight is usually far enough above the take-off weight

I THINK YOU'LL FIND THEY CHECK IN ON TIME NOW !! . . . .

limitation not to be significant, but in order to squeeze the last piece of performance out of the operation, and if the runway threshold is a long way from the terminal, the Captain may load the aircraft right up to the maximum taxi weight. This assumes that enough fuel will be burned before reaching the end of the runway for the weight to be reduced to the maximum allowed for take-off. On one occasion, when I was operating a non-stop Rio de Janeiro to London flight (6,000 miles), I had had the aircraft refuelled to the maximum taxi weight, when five unexpected passengers appeared. It takes a very long time to defuel an aircraft and because the fuel may be contaminated, it has to be put in a discrete bowser. This is an expensive exercise. If the extra passengers were to be accommodated, the aircraft was too heavy even to be pushed back off the stand! The only alternative was to start an engine and burn the fuel before moving, which caused a delay, but a relatively short one.

The maximum take-off weight is a structural one and may be further restricted by the strength, length or slope of the runway, the wind direction and speed, terrain close to the climb-out path, noise abatement considerations (especially at night), aerodrome altitude and/or high ambient temperatures, which reduce engine thrust by affecting the density of the air entering the compressors. All these factors are taken care of in charts or graphs available to the Captain and First Officer, and a calculation is made for every take-off.

The maximum landing weight is that at which the aircraft can be put down without risk of structural damage, and may not be reached until the aircraft has been airborne for several hours and has burned off a significant amount of fuel. In the event of an emergency however, the aircraft may be landed at maximum take-off weight, but will require major engineering checks before it flies again. The wheel brakes are also likely to overheat as a result of dissipating so much energy. This is why, if an aircraft develops a fault after take-off which dictates that it return to its departure point but is not a dire emergency, it is taken to a suitable area for dumping fuel and the weight is reduced to a level suitable for landing. Fuel is emptied from the tanks via outlets specifically for the purpose and can be reduced at up to four tonnes a minute. Ideally this would be over the sea, but if the aircraft is climbed to 6000 feet or above, the fuel will evaporate before reaching the ground and ruining the neighbours' washing.

Pre-flight checks

When they have completed their briefing, the pilots file a Flight Plan with Air Traffic Control (ATC). This consists of a request to fly on a particular route at a particular Flight Level. Place and time of departure are included, plus the speed of the aircraft, so that the controllers can estimate the time that the aircraft will pass each point along its route to its destination. For the purpose of Flight Plans and Telex signals, airports are designated by four-letter codes, such as EGLL (Europe, Great Britain, London (Heathrow), VTBD (Area Victor (South East Asia), Thailand,

Bangkok, Don Muang Airport), etc. Other important information on the Flight Plan includes the alternates the Captain may elect to use in the event of a diversion, the fuel endurance in hours and minutes, and the number of souls on board (there are sometimes tasteless remarks when carrying human remains!). ATC at the aerodrome of departure forwards these details to the destination and all control authorities en route. At busy airports, a departure time 'slot' will be allotted and, just before take-off, a clearance will be issued to the aircraft by radio. If the aircraft is not ready for departure and loses its 'slot', it goes back down the queue and serious delays can occur, though this can sometimes be obviated by the Captain accepting a lower Flight Level than planned or a modified routing (one reason for contingency fuel or a bit extra 'for the wife and kids').

The Flight Crew go out to the aircraft, where the Cabin Attendants are already checking the on-board safety equipment and supervising the loading of catering. As a simple precaution against the possibility of food poisoning affecting more than one of them, each Flight Crew member is provided with a different meal. (In flight, after the passengers have been fed and watered, the crew will be served with high-quality food, usually including some fruit and a cheese tray. They make the most of it. The Cabin Crew may tell you of the time when a First Officer fell into a piranha tank. He ate all he could and took the rest home in his briefcase).

The ground engineer will be refuelling the aircraft to the Captain's requirement. The tank contents are measured by dripsticks (upside-down dipsticks using a magnetic float), crosschecked against the gauges in the Flight Deck, and confirmed by the uplift figure being added to the fuel remaining after the previous flight (recorded in the Technical Log). The engineer also checks tyre pressures, engine oil and hydraulic reservoir contents, destroys the previous Captain's collection of bugs on the windscreen and carries out numerous other routine checks. Incidentally, to prevent the windscreen misting up as a result of the difference in temperature between the inside and outside of the aircraft, a thin layer of electrically heated gold is installed between two layers of Perspex. The gold is so thin that it is transparent. The inner panel takes the strain of the pressurisation of the aircraft in flight, so that if the outer one is cracked, say by impact with a bird, the damage is not necessarily serious, unless the visibility of one of the pilots is adversely affected.

In winter, the ground engineer will be responsible for any de-icing that has to be carried out. This is of vital importance, because ice distorts the smooth flow of air over the wings and thus significantly reduces the lift they generate. It also adds considerable weight. He will have ensured that the Auxiliary Power Unit is running. This is a jet engine located in the tail, big enough to power an executive aircraft but in this case only used to provide electric power and air conditioning before the main engines are started. It ensures that pre-flight checks can be carried out, catering is kept hot when appropriate, and the cabin temperature is comfortable when the passengers board.

The toilets will have been serviced as soon as the aircraft docked from its previous flight. The equipment used for this task is known as the 'honey cart'. Freight, baggage and mail are being loaded under the supervision of the Head Loader, following the instructions of the Dispatcher (who wears a red hat-cover - lady Dispatchers sometimes have to endure a ribbing over this!).

On arrival at the aircraft, the Captain will brief the senior cabin attendant about anything which might concern his team, in particular if turbulence is to be expected (it usually occurs just as coffee is being served after a meal!). He may then have a look at the Technical Log, even if it is not yet ready for his signature, perhaps because refuelling has not been completed. Next he will carry out an external walk-round check of the aircraft, possibly returning via the passenger cabin. Meanwhile, the First Officer settles into the Flight Deck to complete the pre-flight checks and set up the navigation computers and radio ais for departure. His scan of the panels is carried out by memory using a standardised flow pattern, so that nothing is missed. The pilots usually share leg and leg about, during which their roles are reversed. This is the Captain's decision and usually depends on whether it is raining, in which case the First Officer is detailed to carry out the external check (!), but is compensated by being given the take-off and landing. Both pilots therefore are kept in constant practice at handling the aircraft. (Landing technique is to fly the aircraft close to the ground until the non-handling pilot calls upon the deity; the handling pilot then pulls the control column rearwards. This is why First Officers' landings are better than Captains' – the latter are more experienced at calling on the deity at exactly the right moment).

One morning my wife boarded a full aircraft with the other passengers, but had been allocated a 'jump seat' in the Flight Deck. The Chief Steward asked her to wait a short while in the galley outside as the crew were busy with pre-flight checks, and, to make conversation, asked her if she had met me before. She was not quite quick enough to reply that she had shared a bed with me the night before!

The initial cockpit set-up checks are carried out from memory. Subsequently, everything is done by printed checklist on a question and response basis. Each pilot satisfies himself that tasks have been achieved before moving on down the list. Even though these checks may have been done hundreds of times before, self-discipline dictates that the list is followed scrupulously.

The ground engineer will present the Technical Log for the Captain's signature, and, when the aircraft is ready for departure, the Dispatcher brings the Load and Balance Sheet. The doors are closed and the Captain requests start-up clearance from Air Traffic Control. This is given about fifteen minutes before an anticipated take-off time. Clearance to push back off the stand is obtained from Ground Control and the tractor driver gets to work. If you have ever tried to reverse a car with a caravan attached into a restricted space, imagine the skill required to do this with a large aircraft! Meanwhile the engines are turned over by an electric starter or by compressed air from the Auxiliary Power Unit, fuel is introduced and ignited by high-energy sparking plugs, and they spool up to a self-sustaining speed.

When the aircraft is clear of the stand, the tractor is disconnected. Taxi clearance is requested and the handling pilot applies a small amount of power, ensuring that the jet efflux does not dislodge ground equipment and personnel. The aircraft moves gently forward. Steering is by turning the nosewheel with a discrete hydraulically-operated control. This has to be done sensitively, taking into consideration the momentum of a fully-laden aircraft. Particular care has to be taken on an icy taxiway, and it always has to be borne in mind that the main wheels are more than 100 feet behind the Flight Deck, so corners must not be cut or the undercarriage leaves the concrete. Fast taxying is discouraged and the guide speed is 'a fast walking pace'. In practice this has to be interpreted as 'what looks like a fast walking pace' (from the Flight Deck), or it could take half an hour to reach the downwind end of a runway at some of the larger airports! This would make the 32-minute flight between London and Paris extend to an hour and a half!

Pre-take-off checks are carried out, including the selection of wing flaps to a position which enhances lift without unduly increasing drag. The flying controls are checked for full and free movement.

The Air Traffic Control clearance is passed to the pilots and read back meticulously. This will include an appropriate departure route, usually one of several published for the airfield, and may restrict the aircraft to an intermediate Flight Level, further clearance being given when airborne. In the event of a total radio failure, the aircraft is expected to comply with its clearance and subsequently with its filed Flight Plan. Other aircraft will be vectored to maintain separation.

When the runway and the approach path are clear, the aircraft is authorised to line up, and when Departure Control are ready to receive it, it is cleared for take-off.

4

Take-off, Climb and Cruise

Some people think that the purpose of the wings of an aeroplane is to keep the red light on the port tip away from the green light on the starboard one. (Incidentally, a convenient way to remember which is which, is: 'Drink up the *red port left* in the bottle').

Lift depends on the size of the wings and their thickness (the chord), and the volume of air passing over them, a function of speed and air density. The size of the wings can be increased by extending flaps from the trailing edge and lift further enhanced by the use of slats, slots or droop at the leading edge to change the effective chord. All in all a lot of clever ironmongery is employed. For take-off the aircraft is accelerated to a speed at which enough lift is generated for it to leave the ground. How much is enough depends on the weight and the high-lift devices. The Trident, operated mainly by British European Airways (BEA) in the 1960s and 70s, had a very thin wing designed for high speed in the cruise but this resulted in a rather poor aerodrome performance. It was nicknamed the 'Bealine Groundhugger' by pilots and was reputed to get airborne only because of the curvature of the Earth. One pilot reported that, at the far end of Heathrow's main runway, there was a small hut, and on the door was a notice saying 'Keep Out'!

An airliner setting out on a short journey with a relatively small fuel load should only need to reach, say, 140 miles an hour, and thus require a much shorter runway than one operating a long-range flight. The latter will be a lot heavier and may need to achieve something nearer 200 miles an hour. It will take some 40 to 45 seconds and a couple of miles of runway to get there.

The thrust produced by the engines is dependent upon the density of the air entering the compressors, which itself is a function of altitude and temperature. This is why long-haul flights departing from hot countries are usually scheduled at night. With lower temperatures, enough thrust can be generated to accelerate the aircraft to a high enough speed within the length of the runway to generate the lift required for the weight of fuel for the long journey. The maximum weight for a take-off from any particular runway is calculated from tables by the pilots. Obviously in the event of an engine malfunction, it may be necessary to abandon the take-off and the tables also provide the speed up to which the aircraft can safely be stopped by the end of the runway. This is called V1, or velocity 1. If the aircraft has exceeded V1 when a malfunction occurs, the take-off is continued. The aircraft's climb-out performance is certified on the assumption that an engine fails completely at V1. This is where a small four-engined feederliner such as the BAe 146 is so useful, because the loss of one engine is relatively insignificant and therefore it can operate from very short runways.

The next important speed is VR or velocity rotate. This is the speed at which the nose is gently raised, increasing the angle between the airflow and the wings (the angle of attack), which provides enough lift for the aircraft to leave the ground. There is an important contribution to lift caused by the aircraft's proximity to the ground. The air under the wings is bounded by a solid surface beneath, increasing its effectiveness. By the time this is lost, the speed has increased to V2, at which any swing caused by loss of thrust on one side is fully controllable.

Should the take-off be abandoned from a high speed, it will take a considerable time for the wheel brakes to cool, because a huge amount of energy has been dissipated through them. So if a minor malfunction occurs, the take-off is usually only aborted from speeds up to 80 knots (92 miles per hour). Aborting a take-off between 80 knots and V1 would normally only be done for an engine fire or failure.

At light weights and on long runways, the full power available from the engines may not be used. This reduces wear and helps to keep noise at a minimum, something of which pilots are very conscious.

After leaving the ground and when a positive climb is established, the undercarriage is raised to reduce drag. The pilot then sets up a steep climb to 1,000 feet for noise abatement purposes. The idea is to cross the airfield boundary as high as possible. Noise monitoring stations are positioned off the end of the runway. At this point, power is reduced to the continuous climb rating, speed is increased and the wing flaps and other high lift devices are retracted. The aircraft is now clean and accelerates rapidly. There may be a speed restriction applied by Air Traffic Control, and below 10,000 feet consideration must be given to staying below about 320 miles per hour because of the possibility of a bird strike on the Flight Deck windows. (I once saw a large bird flying at 18,000 feet, having been carried up by a thunderstorm over Sicily. This amazed a veterinary surgeon to whom I mentioned it).

Once the aircraft is established in the climb, the forward speed can be increased to perhaps 370 miles an hour whilst still maintaining, at least initially, a rate of climb approaching 2,000 feet per minute. This rate drops off with altitude and it takes between twenty minutes and half an hour to reach a cruising altitude of 33,000 feet.

The Cruise

The airspeed indicator measures the pressure of the air on the nose of the aircraft, sensed through a pitot (pronounced peetoe) tube (not a pilot tube, as often mistakenly assumed by inexperienced typists trying to read a pilot's handwriting!). As altitude is increased, the density of the air decreases, so at a constant indicated airspeed the aircraft is actually accelerating as it climbs. At cruising level the Indicated Airspeed may be 280 knots when the True Air Speed is 480 knots (550 miles per hour). This is one reason why it pays to fly at higher levels. The other is that the engines are much more efficient. Although air density decreases with altitude, a more significant effect on engine performance comes from a balancing effect on density resulting from the drop in temperature. On average air temperature drops by 2° Celsius per thousand feet. Assuming a surface temperature of 15° C, the ambient temperature at 33,000 feet should theoretically be minus 51°. Of course it varies from day to day and season to season. On a very long flight it can be low enough for long enough to chill the fuel in the wings to near the point where it turns to wax, which doesn't flow through the pumps and filters very well! So hot air is ducted from the engine compressors through fuel heaters to ensure that this doesn't happen.

Speed in the cruise is compared with the ambient speed of pressure waves through the air, in other words that at which sound travels (Mach 1). This varies with air density and it is really a convenient way of referring to the speed at which compressibility effects set in, resulting in a rapid increase in drag and the generation of a sonic bang. What needs to be avoided is the increased speed of the air forced to flow round protrusions from the airframe exceeding the critical level, so the cruise is restricted to, for example, Mach 0·84.

Unless restricted by meteorological factors, visibility at cruising level is anything up to 300 miles, particularly when looking at mountains such as Mont Blanc or Mount Teide (Tenerife).

With a view to clearing an aircraft to climb visually through his Flight Level, Air Traffic Control once asked an American pilot what the visibility was. With a southern drawl, he replied, 'Weeell, I can see the Sun, so I guess it's 96 million miles.'

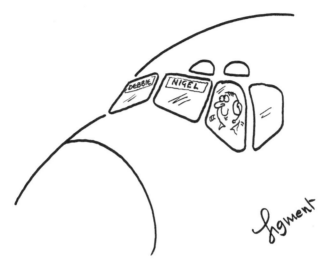

Visitors to the Flight Deck have sometimes remarked that the pilots don't seem to do much, but this is the whole point! At nine miles a minute it is no good just keeping up with the aircraft – you have to be ahead of it. You should not be behaving like a one-armed paperhanger! The whole flight has been carefully pre-planned and the pilots are simply ensuring that the plan is developing along the intended path. What they are doing is managing an extremely complex machine. It is a maxim worth taking seriously that a good pilot uses all his skill and experience to ensure that he never has to use all his skill and experience.

There is in fact plenty to do in the cruise. A check on fuel consumption and remaining tank contents should be made at least every hour. The fuel is contained in a series of tanks in the wings and, for long-range flights, in the lower fuselage. Although about three-quarters of the weight of water, fuel is still a heavy item and needs to be used equally from each side to avoid upsetting the lateral trim of the aircraft. Fuel can reach the engines by gravity feed but is usually helped on its way by booster pumps in each tank. Crossfeed pipes and valves controlled from the Flight Deck allow fuel in any tank to feed any engine, so that, in the event of one engine being shut down, an imbalance between the wings can be avoided and all the fuel carried is available for use. The wings are designed to flex upwards, so that a fuselage carrying a lot of fuel (much heavier than the passenger load) is supported by sloping wings. The fuel in the fuselage is used first and that at the wingtips last so that, as it is consumed and weight is reduced, the wings return more nearly to a horizontal position. (There is always a slight upwards slope (dihedral) to assist the stability of the aircraft as it flies. If it rolls and slips sideways, the angle between the upwind wing and the airflow is greater than that on the downwind side, there is more lift and the aircraft rights itself automatically).

QUI A DIT MERDE ······

All engine instruments should be constantly monitored and readings logged at regular intervals for maintenance purposes. These checks, plus built-in automatically-recording monitoring computers, ensure that any tendency of the engines to lose performance can be picked up and corrected immediately. There are several other systems vital to the operation of the aircraft – hydraulics, pressurisation and air conditioning, de-icing, electrical generation and distribution, flight instruments and the correct order of fuel usage are perhaps the most important. All these have to be watched by skilled and alert eyes, although strident aural warnings are provided for any serious malfunctions. Weather reports for destination, alternates and airports en route can be received from stations broadcasting them continuously or at least every half hour. On the latest aircraft a print-out of them can be obtained from the Automated Message System, saving crew time and attention. There is also a Crew Alert System, providing an aural and visual warning every 15 to 20 minutes, in case the pilots slip into a period of inattention. (Crossing a dozen time-zones in a couple of days makes this a possibility in the early hours of the morning, however hard the crew try to combat it).

At the same time, the accurate navigation of the aircraft has to be achieved. A minute lost costs directly about £166 on a 747. Routine position reports are made to Air Traffic Control (ATC) at designated points, to ensure safe separation from other aircraft. A careful eye is kept on the weather at en route airports, destination and alternates. As fuel is burned and weight reduced, clearance for a climb to a higher level should be sought from ATC to improve engine performance and reduce fuel consumption. However, it is not prudent to climb too high too soon. A clean aircraft (flaps and other high-lift devices retracted) can approach the stall at as high an indicated airspeed (effective airflow over the wings) as 220 knots at very high weights. At high altitude, the maximum cruise Mach number can equate to perhaps as low an indicated airspeed as 235 knots, leaving a very narrow operating range (known as 'suicide corner' for obviously very good reason!).

At least one crew member listens out constantly on the International Emergency frequency (121·5 megahertz). Automatic distress beacons broadcast on this frequency, as well as anybody making emergency calls, which could be relayed to ATC from remote areas. This applies to ships and light aircraft, as well as larger ones.

Very few war-time pilots spoke of their experiences, but one day, when I was a First Officer on Viscounts, we were en route to Gibraltar and were an hour or so into the five-hour flight, when I remarked somewhat wearily to the Captain that it was a long way to Gib. The skipper replied that it took a damned sight longer to walk! It transpired that he had been shot down over the Brest Peninsula (over which we were flying at the time) and walked all the way through France to the Spanish border, thence to the Rock and repatriation. We had another Captain who, in the 1960s, refused to switch on his navigation lights when operating over Germany!

Because of the heavy flow of traffic on the North Atlantic, special arrangements are made to handle it expeditiously. Every twelve hours, a series of tracks is selected according to the forecast en route winds, with reporting points where they cross every 10° of longitude. They are a compromise between the shortest distance (the Great Circle track) and the least headwind westbound, and the best tailwind eastbound. Because of the commercial timing of flights, during the day there may be only one track eastbound but six westbound, all separated from each other laterally. Some go a long way north and are more suited to flights to Chicago and the west coast of the United States and Canada.

I take as an example a flight from London Heathrow to New York Kennedy. The crew will have selected the North Atlantic Track (NATRAC) which is most suitable for the flight and the Flight Level most appropriate to the weight of the aircraft – say, Track Charlie at Flight Level 330 (33,000 feet). They will also have requested the best route on airways from departure to joining the track at its entry point at 8° West. They receive an initial clearance on airways before take-off and proceed accordingly. A transponder on board replies automatically to interrogation from ATC radar, signalling the radio callsign and altitude or Flight Level of the aircraft, which read out on the controller's screen.

By the time they are climbing through 10,000 feet the crew are able to contact Shanwick (the joint Shannon/Prestwick Oceanic Control) and request their clearance across the Atlantic. The Flight Plan they filed on the ground will have been passed to Shanwick, with their choice of NATRAC and optimum cruising level. They will, for example, request 'Track Charlie, Flight Level 330 at Mach Decimal 84'. Shanwick will try to offer this, but if another aircraft is already occupying that track and Flight Level and is not far enough ahead, they will be unable to do so, and will perhaps offer a lower Flight Level (the aircraft will probably be too heavy at this stage to climb to a higher one). The pilots may well then ask them to 'investigate Track Delta', which might offer a crossing at a lateral separation from Track Charlie at the optimum Flight Level with only a small time and fuel penalty. If the air is particularly crowded, as it sometimes is, the crew may have to accept a drastic change to their original plan and coast out, say, over Northern Ireland rather than the Western Isles taking a route well south of their original plan. If by the time they get their transatlantic clearance, the pilots are approaching Manchester, they may have to reprogramme their navigation computer pretty swiftly.

The NATRAC will specify latitudes at which to cross every ten degrees of longitude and the point at which to cross the Canadian coast. Position reports are required at each of these so that Shanwick (and, after 30° West, Gander (Newfoundland) Control) can ensure that separation from other traffic is maintained. Reports are made on High Frequency (HF) single sideband radio until Gander is picked up on the line-of-sight VHF channel about 250 miles out. When the aircraft has burnt enough fuel to reduce its weight substantially, it makes for economy if it is climbed to a higher level. This may be possible under procedural control over the Atlantic and will almost certainly be so once the flight is identified on radar near the coast.

In the event of strong solar activity (sun spots), which peak every eleven years, communication by HF radio can be impossible. I experienced this eastbound one night in the late 1980s, being unable to make routine position reports for more than two hours. We were, from time to time, able to have information relayed to Iceland Control by other aircraft on VHF, whence it was forwarded by landline to Gander and Shanwick. The system fell back on basic procedure and there was no breach of separation standards in spite of heavy traffic.

Crews can talk to those of other aircraft on a discrete VHF frequency, 123·45 megahertz, so that they can pass on weather and other operational information. The North Atlantic is now certainly not a lonely place, but in the days before satellite photographs pinpointed weather systems, the crews of weather ships (long ago withdrawn) on station for months on end were glad of a brief chat.

After crossing the Canadian coast, air traffic diverges according to destination but is joined by domestic flights. The airways are busy but always safely controlled under radar. The Canadians control the aircraft across New Brunswick and hand over to the Americans at the border. Descent into New York begins around Boston. Traffic is often very heavy and delays quite common. Rumour has it that there were originally three Wright Brothers. One of them is still in the stack at Kennedy.

63

5

Descent, Approach and Landing

The descent from cruising level is normally begun at around 140 miles (230km) from destination and planned to achieve a rate of descent of 2,000 feet per minute, with the engines at idle power – effectively almost a glide, though there will be some residual thrust. This is a comfortable rate and allows the cabin to be depressurised at about 300 feet per minute which should not cause any discomfort to the ears of passengers. Winds change considerably with height and the achievement of the correct descent profile is carefully monitored by the pilots. Arrival at the entry to the terminal area too high and too fast, leads to a very hurried and untidy approach; reaching the bottom of descent too early is extremely wasteful of fuel and time as fuel consumption at a low altitude is high and the true air speed decreases with height.

If the inbound route also has outbound aircraft on it, the descent may have to be interrupted until opposing traffic has passed underneath. If this modification is significant, the rate of descent will have to be increased. This can be achieved by deploying speedbrakes – panels which come out from the top of the wing, spoiling the airflow and thus reducing lift. This often causes some vibration. The rate of descent can be increased to 4,000 feet per minute or more.

As a busy terminal area is reached, a speed restriction (usually 250 knots) is often imposed. This equalises the rate at which the various types of aircraft progress, and allows the air traffic controllers more easily to separate inbound traffic under radar control. As aircraft cannot stop without falling out of the sky, it is sometimes necessary to direct them into a holding pattern, stacked up at 1,000-foot intervals in the queue. The pattern is based on a radio beacon on the ground and is in the form of a racetrack.

The aim is to fly the racetrack pattern as accurately as possible (otherwise the aircraft may stray into adjacent traffic flows) and to return to the beacon in six minutes exactly. In theory, the aircraft should take one minute to turn through 180°, fly for two minutes on that heading, take another minute to turn back through 180° again and complete the hold in two further minutes. This will happen if there is no wind. In practice, the pilot has to make an allowance on the outbound leg for any crosswind effect on the leg itself but also for its effect throughout the two turns. He does this by doubling the drift experienced. The aircraft should, if the pilot has exercised enough skill, roll out on the correct inbound track. He then has to allow for the drift as he flies into the beacon. At the same time as all this, he has to allow for the wind effect on speed on both straight legs and both turns, adjusting the time on the outbound leg up or down, so that the pattern is completed in exactly six minutes. The pilot may have to change altitude in the pattern, as aircraft beneath him are cleared to make an approach, so he is working in three dimensions. Accurate flying here is essential and is practised regularly on the simulator as well as for real on the line.

So that the controller does not have to repeat to each aircraft the same aerodrome information (surface wind, temperature, visibility, cloud base, precipitation, etc.), this is continuously broadcast on a discrete frequency and given a phonetic alphabet codename (Information Delta, for example). A pilot can receive this on a radio set not being used for two-way communication so that, on first calling the Approach Controller, he can advise him that he has the information by its codename. The broadcast is changed every half hour or so, or more frequently if necessary.

The last few miles before landing are called the approach. When the aircraft's turn comes to make an approach, it is cleared to leave the holding pattern on a heading to intercept the extended centreline of the runway at eight to twelve miles out. This may initially be at right angles and is adjusted to allow a smooth transition on to the centreline which, at well-equipped airports, is designated by an Instrument Landing System (ILS). This is a radio transmission which gives the pilot a 'fly left/fly right' indication on an instrument on his panel, to enable him to track down the centreline. There is also a Glideslope transmission, which gives him a 'fly up/fly down' signal so that he can make a steady approach at an angle of 3°, giving a rate of descent, depending on the wind, of about 700 feet per minute at around 300 feet per mile over the ground. Wing flaps are lowered to allow the aircraft to fly more slowly by effectively increasing the size of the wing and its camber (thickness), achieving more lift at a lower speed. A fair amount of power is applied to counteract the extra drag generated. The throttles can be set to maintain a selected airspeed automatically. The undercarriage is usually lowered at 2,000 feet above the ground, seven miles out. Of course, a good landing begins in the Briefing Room before take-off, and a nice unhurried, steady approach will clinch it.

The Ground Proximity Warning System (GPWS), detecting the rate of closure with the ground, is active during all phases of the flight. An enhanced version, using technology developed by the US military for cruise missiles, uses satellite navigation and a mapping database to provide the crew with a picture of the terrain they are overflying. The system provides a strident warning should the separation between the aircraft and the ground become dangerously reduced. It also monitors the rate of descent during the approach. The parameters are reduced as the aircraft nears the ground but if the rate of descent is inappropriate, a clear aural 'WHOOP, WHOOP - PULL UP' warning is generated. In the event of this being triggered, the pilot must apply full power and initiate an immediate 'go around', asking questions later.

Should there be low cloud or fog, the ILS puts the pilot in the perfect position to take over visually at his approach limit, usually 200 feet above the ground at just under 1200 yards (1100 m) from the touchdown point. (This latter should be 1000 feet down the runway, to ensure adequate wheel height over the threshold). Even if he cannot see the runway itself from 200 feet, he will be able safely to continue his approach if the centreline and crossbars of the approach lights leading to the runway give him strong visual information as to whether his wings are level and he is on the centreline. He also has useful assistance from Visual Approach Slope Indicators (VASIs). These consist of two bars of lights on either side of the runway, usually positioned at 150 metres and 300 metres beyond the threshold. Each bar is divided horizontally into two segments which show white lights on the high side and red ones on the low. The pilot of an aircraft on the correct approach path will see white lights nearest him and red ones on the further bars, indicating that he is high for the nearer lights and low for the further ones. If he drifts high, he will see two sets of white lights, and a low approach will be signalled by two groups of red ones. For long-bodied aircraft, on which the landing gear can be fifteen feet below the pilot's eye level in the nose-up attitude of the approach, an extra set of lights is installed, so that a safe wheel height above the runway threshold is assured. The pilot uses the second and third pairs of bars, instead of the first and second.

The aircraft is flown to within a few feet of the ground at around 130 to 140 miles an hour, depending on its weight, when the rate of descent is decreased by gently raising the nose (the flare). The throttles are closed and the aircraft touches down at just above the stalling speed. If it is stalled on to the ground, the aircraft will arrive with an undignified crunch. If the touchdown is too fast and the aircraft therefore still has flying speed, it will bounce, leaving the pilot with the whole thing to do over again, or, if the bounce is a high one, the need to apply full power and go around for another approach. The wheels are stationary when they touch the runway and have to spin up to the speed of the aircraft instantly, hence the puff of smoke seen on touchdown. Nevertheless, the tyres will normally last for a hundred landings or so. Fitting electric or hydraulic motors to spin them up prior to landing would not be practical because of the extra weight involved, and because, as the wind determines the groundspeed of the aircraft, it would be impossible to match exactly the wheel speed with the touchdown speed.

When the wheels are in contact with the runway, the speedbrakes deploy automatically (triggered by 'weight-on' switches on the undercarriage), killing the lift and increasing drag to assist in slowing the aircraft. The pilot selects reverse thrust on the engines. This is achieved by buckets dropping into the jet efflux and deflecting the thrust outwards and forwards at about 45°. On short or wet runways, power is increased to achieve more retardation, but 'reverse idle' only may be selected to keep noise at a minimum, especially at airports close to residential areas.

When landing on runways with standing water, consideration must be given to the possibility of aquaplaning, where the wheels are not actually in contact with the runway but ride on a thin layer of water building up in front of them. This will substantially reduce retardation and, if the wheels are not turning, generate steam between them and the runway, scalding the rubber off the tyres. Aquaplaning can occur at any speed above nine times the square root of the tyre pressure—about 100 miles an hour for a large aircraft. Compare this with a car, where aquaplaning is possible at anything over 45 to 50 miles per hour (if you see no wheel tracks on a wet road in your rear-view mirror, you could be aquaplaning!). In the event of a wet-runway landing, it is therefore good airmanship to ensure a firm touchdown, to allow the wheels to break through the water layer. So don't necessarily criticise the pilot – he may have done it purposely! Aircraft are fitted with anti-skid brakes, which ensure the best possible retardation.

In the event of a crosswind, the aircraft is tracked down the extended centreline of the runway by heading slightly into wind. If this were to be maintained to touchdown, the wheels would drop on to the runway sideways, causing undue stress on the undercarriage legs, so the pilot kicks the aircraft straight with the rudder at just the right moment. Too soon and the aircraft drifts towards the downwind edge of the runway, too late and it touches down still pointing into wind but tracking down the runway.

An alternative method of dealing with a crosswind is to bank into it and touch down on one wheel, subsequently kicking the aircraft straight with the rudder. This is not really suitable for large jet aircraft, because the whole weight of the aircraft is on one undercarriage leg and, especially if the nose is allowed to rise, there is the chance of one of the engines contacting the runway. As they cost around £6 million pounds each, this is not recommended! It is rather a lot to be deducted from your pay at the end of the month!

The autopilot (a set of gyroscopes or spinning tops with electronic input to modify their performance) can be engaged to track the ILS for a highly accurate approach, and at suitably-equipped airports can achieve automatic landings more safely than those of a Mark 1 human being. It is therefore certified for approaches and landings down to very low cloud base and visibility minima indeed, typically 75 metres runway visual range and cloud on the surface. Three autopilots are engaged to provide cross-monitoring and the way in which the approach, flare and landing is developing can be carefully monitored by the pilots. The autopilot disconnect button (nicknamed the 'chicken switch') is on the control column and a finger is poised over it at all times. A 'go-around' can be initiated at any time, even after touchdown.

The first aircraft to have this equipment built in right from the start, as opposed to being retro-fitted, was the Lockheed L-1011 TriStar. I was involved as a line pilot in the long development program before this was certified for use down to lower than visual limits. A significant factor is the unique fitting on the TriStar of Direct Lift Control. When wing flaps are selected out at the beginning of the approach the speedbrakes deploy to 7°. Pitch input into the control column, either from the pilot or the autopilot, deploys them more or less, decreasing or increasing the lift, rather than changing the pitch angle of the aircraft via the elevators, which is much slower to take effect. This achieves a delightfully smooth and accurate control of the descent down the glideslope.

Radio altimeters (which measure the exact height of the aircraft above the ground by bouncing radio waves off it and measuring the time it takes for the signal to return) are used to achieve the flare, leaving the pilots only the tasks of selecting reverse thrust on touchdown and applying the wheelbrakes. If the autopilot is left engaged, the aircraft will track down the centreline of the runway until it stops. The pilot can then take over and taxi the aircraft to the terminal. Landing visibility limits are only restricted by the ability of the pilot to see down from the flight deck and far enough forward to taxi safely.

As the aircraft taxies in, there is always an announcement asking passengers to remain seated until the aircraft stops and the engines have been shut down. On almost every flight passengers defy this safety instruction. In the event that the wheelbrakes have to be applied suddenly, any standing passengers would be catapulted forward with a very good chance of breaking a limb or neck. Any insurance claim would be instantly rejected. As it will take several minutes to file off the aircraft and probably a wait of twenty minutes or so for the baggage to be offloaded and carried to the carousel in the terminal, such behaviour is not only stupid but utterly pointless. The pilots' shutdown checks include the switching off of the 'Fasten Seat Belts' sign, so why not wait a few seconds for this to be done?

After you have been looked after by highly-trained professionals in the air and on the ground, you are now exposed to a far more dangerous part of your journey, the ride from the airport amongst amateur drivers with lots of bad habits and possibly in poorly-maintained vehicles. That's worth thinking about!

SEE IF THEY'VE GOT A CLEARANCE YET
WILL YOU, ONLY I RETIRE ON TUESDAY

Appendix 1

International Aircraft Registration Prefixes

AP	Pakistan	ER	Moldova
A2	Botswana	ES	Estonia
A3	Tonga	ET	Ethiopia
A4O	Oman	EW	Belarus
A5	Bhutan	EX	Kyrgyzstan
A6	United Arab Emirates	EY	Tajikistan
A7	Qatar	EZ	Turkmenistan
A9C	Bahrain	E3	Eritrea
B	People's Republic of China	F	France
B	Republic of China (Taiwan)		
B-H	Hong Kong, People's Republic of China	G	United Kingdom
C	Canada	HA	Hungary
CC	Chile	HB	Switzerland and Liechtenstein
CCCP	Soviet Union (now obsolete)		
CN	Morocco	HC	Ecuador
CP	Bolivia	HH	Haiti
CS	Portugal	HI	Dominican Republic
CU	Cuba	HK	Colombia
CX	Uruguay	HL	Republic of Korea
C2	Nauru	HP	Panama
C5	Gambia	HR	Honduras
C6	Bahamas	HS	Thailand
C9	Mozambique	HZ	Saudi Arabia
		H4	Solomon Islands
D	Germany		
DQ	Fiji	I	Italy
D2	Angola		
D4	Cape Verde	JA	Japan
D6	Comoro	JY	Jordan
		J2	Djibouti
EC	Spain	J3	Grenada
EI	Ireland	J5	Guinea Bissau
EK	Armenia	J6	St Lucia
EL	Liberia	J7	Dominica
EP	Iran	J8	St Vincent

LN	Norway	S7	Seychelles
LV	Argentina	S9	Sao Tome
LX	Luxembourg		
LY	Lithuania	TC	Turkey
LZ	Bulgaria	TF	Iceland
		TG	Guatemala
MT	Mongolia	TI	Costa Rica
		TJ	Cameroon
N	USA	TL	Central African Republic
		TN	Republic of Congo (Congo-Brazzaville)
OB	Peru		
OD	Lebanon	TR	Gabon
OE	Austria	TS	Tunisia
OH	Finland	TT	Chad
OK	Czech Republic	TU	Ivory Coast
OM	Slovakia	TY	Benin
OO	Belgium	TZ	Mali
OY	Denmark	T2	Tuvalu
		T3	Kiribati
P	Democratic Republic of Korea	T9	Bosnia Herzegovina
PH	Netherlands	UK	Uzbekistan
PJ	Netherlands Antilles	UN	Kazakhstan
PK	Indonesia	UR	Ukraine
PP	Brazil		
PZ	Suriname	VH	Australia
P2	Papua New Guinea	VN	Vietnam
P4	Aruba	VP-B	Bermuda
		VP-C	Cayman Islands
RA	Russian Federation	VP-F	Falkland Islands
RDPL	Lao People's Democratic Republic	VP-G	Gibraltar
		VP-LA	Leeward Islands
RP	Philippines	VP-LP	British Virgin Islands
		VQ-T	Turks and Caicos
SE	Sweden	VR-H	Hong Kong (now obsolete)
SP	Poland	VT	India
ST	Sudan	V2	Antigua
SU	Egypt	V3	Belize
SX	Greece	V4	St Kitts and Nevis
S2	Bangladesh	V5	Namibia
S5	Slovenia	V6	Micronesia

V7	Marshall Islands	5H	Tanzania
V8	Brunei	5N	Nigeria
		5R	Madagascar
XA	Mexico	5T	Mauritania
XT	Burkina Faso	5U	Niger
XU	Cambodia	5V	Togo
XY	Myanmar	5W	Western Samoa
		5X	Uganda
YA	Afghanistan	5Y	Kenya
YJ	Vanuatu		
YK	Syria	6O	Somalia
YL	Latvia	6V	Senegal
YN	Nicaragua	6Y	Jamaica
YR	Romania		
YS	El Salvador		
YU	Yugoslavia	7O	Yemen Republic
YV	Venezuela	7P	Lesotho
		7Q	Malawi
Z	Zimbabwe	7T	Algeria
ZA	Albania		
ZK	New Zealand	8Q	Maldives
ZP	Paraguay	8R	Guyana
ZS	South Africa		
Z3	Macedonia	9A	Croatia
		9G	Ghana
3A	Monaco	9H	Malta
3B	Mauritius	9J	Zambia
3C	Equatorial Guinea	9K	Kuwait
3D	Swaziland	9L	Sierra Leone
3X	Guinea	9M	Malaysia
		9N	Nepal
4K	Azerbaijan	9P	Barbados
4L	Georgia	9Q	Democratic Republic of
4R	Sri Lanka		Congo (Zaire)
4X	Israel	9U	Burundi
		9V	Singapore
5A	Libya	9XR	Rwanda
5B	Cyprus	9Y	Trinidad and Tobago

Appendix 2
The Phonetic Alphabet

Current	Pre-1956
Alpha	Able
Bravo	Baker
Charlie	Charlie
Delta	Dog
Echo	Easy
Foxtrot	Fox
Golf	George
Hotel	How
India	Item
Juliet	Jig
Kilo	King
Lima	Love
Mike	Mike
November	Nan
Oscar	Oboe
Papa	Peter
Quebec (pronounced Keebeck)	Queen
Romeo	Roger
Sierra	Sugar
Tango	Tare
Uniform	Uncle
Victor	Victor
Whisky	William
X-Ray	X-Ray
Yankee	Yoke
Zulu	Zebra

Abbreviations

ATC	Air Traffic Control
ATPL	Airline Transport Pilot's Licence
BEA	British European Airways
EGLL	Europe, Great Britain, London (Heathrow)
ETA	Estimated Time of Arrival
ETD	Estimated Time of Departure
GPWS	Ground Proximity Warning System
HF	High Frequency (3,000 to 30,000 kilohertz)
ILS	Instrument Landing System
INS	Inertial Navigational System
IR	Instrument Rating
JAA	Joint Aviation Authority
NATRAC	North Atlantic Track
QFE	Atmospheric Pressure at aerodrome elevation or at runway threshold
QNH	Altimeter Sub-scale Setting for altitudes level (height above sea level)
Shanwick	Shannon/Prestwick Oceanic Control
V1	Velocity 1
V2	Velocity 2
VASI	Visual Approach Slope Indicator
VHF	Very High Frequency (30 to 300 megahertz)
VIP	Very Important Person
VOR	VHF Omni-directional Radio Range
VR	Velocity Rotate
VTPC	Area Victor (South East Asia), Thailand, Bangkok, Don Muang

Index